# 11+ Maths

## For GL Assessment

It's no secret that the GL 11+ test can be seriously tricky. But don't worry — this CGP Practice Book will give children a brilliant headstart on their test preparation.

In the first few sections, they can practise answering questions on one topic at a time. Then, when they're ready for more realistic 11+ practice, give the Assessment Tests a try.

It's all set at just the right level for Ages 8-9, so it's perfect for building their confidence. And with detailed answers included at the back, marking is a breeze!

### How to access your free Online Edition

This book includes a free Online Edition to read on your PC, Mac or tablet.
You'll just need to go to cgpbooks.co.uk/extras and enter this code:

4388 2065 6001 4634

By the way, this code only works for one person. If somebody else has used this book before you, they might have already claimed the Online Edition.

## Practice Book — Ages 8-9

### with Assessment Tests

# How to use this Practice Book

This book is divided into two parts — themed question practice and assessment tests.
There are answers and detailed explanations at the end of the book.

## Themed question practice

- Each page contains practice questions divided by topic. Use these pages to work out your child's strengths and the areas they find tricky. The questions get harder down each page.
- Your child can use the smiley face tick boxes to evaluate how confident they feel with each topic.

## Assessment tests

- The second half of the book contains six assessment tests, each with a mix of question types from the first half of the book. They take a similar form to the real test.
- You can print multiple-choice answer sheets so your child can practise the tests as if they're sitting the real thing — visit cgpbooks.co.uk/11plus/answer-sheets or scan the QR code.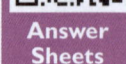
- Use the printable answer sheets if you want your child to do each test more than once.
- If you want to give your child timed practice, give them a time limit of 35 minutes for each test, and ask them to work as quickly and carefully as they can.
- Your child should aim for a mark of around 85% (26 questions correct) in each test. If they score less than this, use their results to work out the areas they need more practice on.
- If they haven't managed to finish the test in time, they need to work on increasing their speed, whereas if they have made a lot of mistakes, they need to work more carefully.
- Keep track of your child's scores using the progress chart at the back of the book.

---

Published by CGP

Editors:
Luke Antieul, David Broadbent, Sharon Keeley-Holden, Sarah Williams

Contributors:
Sue Foord, John Hawkins, Julie Hunt, Katrina Saville

With thanks to Rachel Murray and Glenn Rogers for the proofreading.

ISBN: 978 1 78908 157 2
Printed by Elanders Ltd, Newcastle upon Tyne
Clipart from Corel®

Based on the classic CGP style created by Richard Parsons.

Text, design, layout and original illustrations © Coordination Group Publications Ltd. (CGP) 2018
All rights reserved.

Photocopying this book is not permitted, even if you have a CLA licence.
Extra copies are available from CGP with next day delivery • 0800 1712 712 • www.cgpbooks.co.uk

# Contents

## Section One — Number Knowledge

Place Value ........................................................................... 2
Rounding Up and Down ..................................................... 4
Number Knowledge .............................................................. 6
Number Sequences ............................................................... 8
Fractions ............................................................................... 10
Fractions and Decimals ....................................................... 11

*Tick off the check box for each topic as you go along.*

## Section Two — Working with Numbers

Addition ............................................................................... 12
Subtraction .......................................................................... 14
Multiplying and Dividing by 10 and 100 ........................... 16
Multiplication ..................................................................... 17
Division ............................................................................... 19

## Section Three — Word Problems

Word Problems ................................................................... 21

## Section Four — Data Handling

Data Tables ......................................................................... 23
Displaying Data .................................................................. 25

## Section Five — Shape and Space

Angles .................................................................................. 27
2D Shapes ............................................................................ 28
2D Shapes — Area and Perimeter ...................................... 29
Symmetry ............................................................................. 30
3D Shapes ............................................................................ 31
Shape Problems .................................................................. 32
Coordinates ......................................................................... 33

## Section Six — Units and Measures

Units ..................................................................................... 34
Time ..................................................................................... 35

## Section Seven — Mixed Problems

Mixed Problems .................................................................. 36

## Assessment Tests

Test 1 ................................................................................... 37
Test 2 ................................................................................... 42
Test 3 ................................................................................... 47
Test 4 ................................................................................... 52
Test 5 ................................................................................... 57
Test 6 ................................................................................... 62

Answers ............................................................................... 67
Progress Chart .................................................................... 86

## Place Value

For each row of numbers below, circle the number that is the smallest.

1. 165    95    120    180    50
2. 3000    890    2450    1900    980
3. 120    174    131    114    128
4. 1230    3420    2030    1440    2620
5. 4.2    2.7    3.1    3.5    2.4

/ 5

What number is the arrow pointing to on each of these number lines?

6. (number line from 10 to 20, arrow pointing between 10 and 15)   Answer: _____

7. (number line from 0 to 20, arrow pointing between 0 and 10)   Answer: _____

8. (number line from 45 to 95, arrow pointing between 70 and 95)   Answer: _____

9. (number line from 14 to 24, arrow pointing between 14 and 24)   Answer: _____

10. (number line from 30 to 80, arrow pointing between 30 and 80)   Answer: _____

/ 5

Write down whether the 7 in each of the following numbers stands for hundreds, tens, units, tenths or hundredths.

11. 710    Answer: _____

12. 627.4    Answer: _____

13. 7.36    Answer: _____

14. 26.71    Answer: _____

15. 14.27    Answer: _____

/ 5

# Place Value

16. Rearrange the digits in 2753 to make the largest number possible.

    Answer: _____

17. Josephine timed how long each member of her family spent brushing their teeth. She recorded the results in this table. Who brushed their teeth in the shortest time?

    Answer: _____

    | Name | Time (seconds) |
    |------|----------------|
    | Dad | 138 |
    | Mum | 146 |
    | John | 108 |
    | Natalie | 155 |
    | Karen | 114 |

18. The heights of 5 children were measured. Their heights were 1.21 m, 1.12 m, 1.20 m, 1.02 m and 1.10 m.
    What was the height of the shortest person?   Answer: _____ m

19. Circle the number that is exactly halfway between 2.4 and 3.8.
    A   3.0        B   3.2        C   2.9        D   2.6        E   3.1

20. Mr Pearson is catching a plane. His luggage weighs 20.08 kg. How many of these airlines would let him take his luggage on the plane?

    Answer: _____

    | Airline | Maximum luggage weight (kg) |
    |---------|------------------------------|
    | Air Kings | 20.2 |
    | Fast Flights | 19.95 |
    | Fly by Night | 20.14 |
    | Pronto Planes | 20.4 |
    | Speedy Jet | 20.05 |

21. Which of these pairs of numbers are the same distance from 19? Circle the correct answer.

    A   12 and 24        C   16 and 21        E   14 and 25
    B   17 and 22        D   15 and 23

22. Circle the number which is closest to 1000.
    A   996.7    B   1004.1    C   1002.9    D   996.3    E   997.5

23. 6 is exactly halfway between one of these pairs of numbers. Circle the correct pair.

    A   6.7 and 5.7        C   6.1 and 5.7        E   6.6 and 5.3
    B   6.4 and 5.6        D   6.8 and 5.5

# Rounding Up and Down

Round the following numbers to the nearest 10.

1. 71   Answer: _____

2. 349   Answer: _____

3. 407   Answer: _____

4. 1536   Answer: _____

5. 3092   Answer: _____

/ 5

Round 1295.61 to:

6. the nearest 100.   Answer: _____

7. the nearest tenth.   Answer: _____

8. the nearest 10.   Answer: _____

9. the nearest whole number.   Answer: _____

/ 4

Write down whether these numbers have been rounded to the nearest 10, 100 or 1000:

10. 25 rounded to 30.   Answer: _____

11. 381 rounded to 400.   Answer: _____

12. 615 rounded to 620.   Answer: _____

13. 1247 rounded to 1000.   Answer: _____

14. 517.4 rounded to 500.   Answer: _____

/ 5

15. Anya has £6.27 in her purse. What is £6.27 rounded to the nearest pound?   Answer: £ _____

16. There are 212 fish in an aquarium. How many fish are there to the nearest 10?   Answer: _____

17. 3264 people attended a rugby match. How many is this to the nearest 100?   Answer: _____

/ 3

Section One — Number Knowledge

# Rounding Up and Down

18. Jan runs a market stall. She decides to round all of her prices to the nearest 10p. Which two items will now be cheaper? Circle the correct answer.

    A   potatoes and cauliflower
    B   tomatoes and runner beans
    C   cabbage and tomatoes
    D   runner beans and cauliflower
    E   cabbage and cauliflower

| Item | Price |
|---|---|
| Potatoes | 76p |
| Cauliflower | £1.15 |
| Tomatoes | 93p |
| Runner beans | 47p |
| Cabbage | 84p |

19. The path around Mo's garden is 1265 cm. Round this length to the nearest 10 cm.    Answer: _____ cm

20. A book weighs 159.53 g. What is this weight rounded to the nearest whole number?    Answer: _____ g

21. Josie is 147.5 cm tall and Martina is 145.3 cm tall. They both round their height to the nearest 10 cm. Which of these statements is true? Circle the correct answer.

    A   Josie's rounded height is greater than Martina's rounded height.
    B   Martina and Josie have the same rounded height.
    C   Josie's height is rounded to 148 cm.
    D   Martina's height is rounded to 140 cm.
    E   Martina's height is rounded to 100 cm.

22. The town of Thelston has a population of 6000, rounded to the nearest 1000. Circle the number that could not be the actual number of people living in Thelston.

    A   5621    B   5495    C   6497    D   6010    E   6318

23. Ben's dad weighs 78.49 kg. What is his weight rounded to the nearest 0.1 kg?    Answer: _____ kg

24. Which of these is equal to 650? Circle the correct answer.

    A   626.5 to the nearest 10         D   650.7 to the nearest whole number
    B   6490 to the nearest 100         E   646.1 to the nearest 10
    C   657.2 to the nearest 10

# Number Knowledge

For each row of numbers below, circle the lowest value.

1. 0.7   6   0.2   1   3

2. 3   –6   1   0   –2

Complete each statement using a < or > sign.

3. –5 _____ –9

4. 2 _____ –4

5. –3 _____ 0

Hint: < means 'is less than' and > means 'is greater than'.

/ 5

6. What is 64 in Roman numerals? Circle the correct answer.
   A  CXIV     B  LXIV     C  XLVI     D  DXIV     E  LXVI

7. This table shows the maximum temperature each morning for 5 days. What is the difference between the highest and lowest temperatures recorded?

   Answer: _____ °C

   | Day | Temperature (°C) |
   |---|---|
   | Monday | –3 |
   | Tuesday | 0 |
   | Wednesday | 2 |
   | Thursday | –2 |
   | Friday | –1 |

8. Which of these statements is false? Circle the correct answer.
   A  49 + 17 will give an even number.
   B  34 – 18 will give an even number.
   C  17 + 12 will give an odd number.
   D  6 × 6 will give an even number.
   E  19 – 9 will give an odd number.

9. Jacob starts at –26 and subtracts 22. What number does Jacob end up at?   Answer: _____

10. Which number is in the wrong section of this Venn diagram?

    Answer: _____

    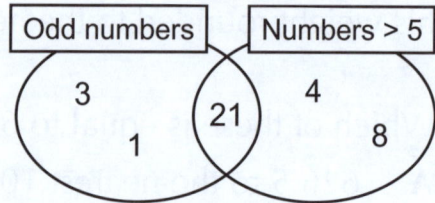

11. Circle the number below that is even and greater than –3.

    1     7     –6     2     5

/ 6

Section One — Number Knowledge

# Number Knowledge

12. Rabin's age is equal to the sum of the first three multiples of 4.  How old is Rabin?     Answer: _____

13. Circle the number that is not a factor of 48.
    **A**  8     **B**  4     **C**  12     **D**  6     **E**  9

14. Circle the number which is a multiple of 6 and 9.
    **A**  30     **B**  12     **C**  18     **D**  27     **E**  3

15. Constance thinks of a number.  It is the sum of all of the odd numbers between 0 and 10.  What is her number?     Answer: _____

16. There are 36 children at a party.  They all split into equal teams to play some games.  Which of these cannot be the number of children in each team?  Circle the correct answer.

    Hint: The number of children on each team must be a factor of 36.

    **A**  6     **B**  3     **C**  4     **D**  9     **E**  8

17. Cathy says that all multiples of 3 are odd numbers.
    Dolly says that all multiples of 4 are even numbers.
    Ellie says that all multiples of 2 are also multiples of 4.
    Which of the statements below is true?  Circle the correct answer.

    **A** Only Ellie is correct.                **D** Ellie and Dolly are both correct.
    **B** Cathy and Dolly are both correct.     **E** Only Dolly is correct.
    **C** Cathy, Dolly and Ellie are all correct.

18. Which set of labels is missing from the sorting table?
    Circle the correct answer.

    |   | odd numbers | even numbers |
    |---|---|---|
    | ? | 3, 5 | 6 |
    | ? | 7 | 4, 8 |

    **A**  factors of 15; not factors of 15
    **B**  multiples of 3; not multiples of 3
    **C**  less than 6; 6 or more
    **D**  factors of 30; not factors of 30
    **E**  less than 5; 5 or more

19. Circle the set of numbers which contains only multiples of 2 or 5.
    2, 10, 13     3, 4, 15     16, 20, 25     12, 13, 14     25, 30, 33

    / 8

# Number Sequences

Write down the next number in each of the sequences below.

1. 7, 10, 13, 16...    Answer: _____

2. 6, 12, 18, 24...    Answer: _____

3. 28, 26, 24, 22...    Answer: _____

4. 8.5, 9, 9.5, 10...    Answer: _____

5. 1, 2, 4, 8...    Answer: _____

The students in Year 4 are making number sequences. What is the 3rd number in each person's sequence?

6. Tariq starts at 2 and counts on in steps of 3.
   Answer: _____

7. Michelle starts at 8 and counts on in steps of 6.
   Answer: _____

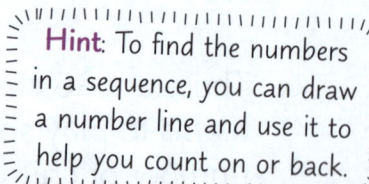

Hint: To find the numbers in a sequence, you can draw a number line and use it to help you count on or back.

8. Harpreet starts at 0 and counts on in steps of 0.5.
   Answer: _____

9. Paul starts at 20 and counts back in steps of 6.
   Answer: _____

10. Gabrielle starts at 36 and counts back in steps of 5.
    Answer: _____

Write down the missing number in each of the sequences below.

11. 5, 10, 15, _____, 25

12. 9, 13, 17, 21, _____

13. 52, _____, 56, 58, 60

14. 45, 42, _____, 36, 33

15. _____, 42, 35, 28, 21

Section One — Number Knowledge

# Number Sequences

16. Klara starts at 18 and counts on in steps of 6.
    Circle the number which will be in her sequence.

    **A** 34    **B** 35    **C** 36    **D** 37    **E** 38

17. The diagram shows the tiles on Mr Aston's roof.
    In each row there is 1 more tile than in the previous row.
    How many tiles will he have in the 6th row?

    Answer: _____

    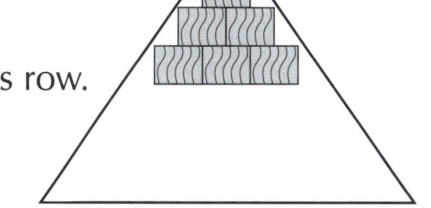

18. Nilesh writes down a sequence starting at 16. He counts back
    in steps of 3. Circle the number that will not be in his sequence.

    7    3    4    1    10

19. Caitlin starts at 10 and counts on in steps of 2.5.
    Circle the number that will be in her sequence.

    16.5    18    17.5    14    13.5

20. Charlie started at 7 and used the rule "subtract 5" to make a sequence.
    What is the 4th number in his sequence? Circle the correct answer.

    **A** −3    **B** −7    **C** 2    **D** −2    **E** −8

21. Jesper writes a sequence of numbers with the rule:
    *Add the last two numbers together.*
    The first five numbers in the sequence are:
         1, 2, 3, 5, 8
    What is the 7th number in Jesper's sequence?     Answer: _____

22. Molly writes a sequence using the rule "add 5". She starts at 2.
    Circle the number that will be in her sequence.

    **A** 27    **B** 28    **C** 29    **D** 30    **E** 31

23. Gina is using a sequence to plant seeds in some plant pots. She plants
    1 seed in the 1st pot, 4 seeds in the 2nd pot, 7 seeds in the 3rd pot
    and so on. Circle the number of seeds she will plant in the 5th pot.

    **A** 9    **B** 10    **C** 7    **D** 13    **E** 12

/ 8

Section One — Number Knowledge

# Fractions

A fraction of each of these shapes is shaded. Write down the letter of the shape that matches each fraction.

1. ½     Answer: _____
2. ¾     Answer: _____
3. ²⁄₆     Answer: _____
4. ⅕     Answer: _____
5. ⅝     Answer: _____

A   B   C   D   E

/ 5

6. There are 16 sweets in a bag. Lakshmi eats ¼ of the sweets. How many sweets does Lakshmi eat?    Answer: _____

7. What fraction of the rectangle is shaded? Circle the correct answer.

    A ³⁄₁₂    B ⁵⁄₁₂    C ⁸⁄₁₂    D ⁷⁄₁₂    E ⁶⁄₁₂

8. Which letter shows where the fraction ¾ should be placed on this number line? Circle the correct answer.

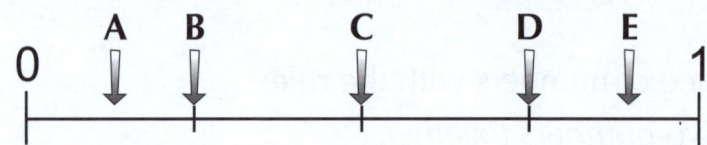

9. A bag of crisps is normally 60p. How much do the crisps cost under this special offer?

    Answer: _____ p

**Special Offer**
Crisps are ⅓ of the normal price.

10. ¼ of the circle on the right is shaded. Which of the circles below has an equal amount shaded? Circle the correct answer.

A    B    C    D    E

*Hint: Fractions with different numerators and denominators can be equal in value.*

/ 5

Section One — Number Knowledge

# Fractions and Decimals

Write the fractions below as decimals.

1. ½   Answer: _____
2. ¼   Answer: _____
3. ¹⁄₁₀   Answer: _____
4. ¾   Answer: _____
5. ⁸⁄₁₀   Answer: _____

/ 5

Circle the largest value in each row.

6. 0.8   ½   0.2   0.75   ¼
7. ⁶⁄₁₀   ¾   ½   0.4   0.5
8. ¼   0.2   0.1   ¹⁄₁₀   ²⁄₁₀

/ 3

9. ⁷⁄₁₀ of this shape is shaded. What is this value as a decimal?

Answer: _____

10. Joyce shared £1.00 with her two sisters. Annette got £0.10, Elizabeth got £0.50 and Joyce kept £0.40. What fraction of the money did Elizabeth get?   Answer: _____

11. Micah eats ²⁄₄ of a pizza and Rose eats ¼. Which of the following decimals shows the amount of pizza left over? Circle the correct answer.

    A   0.2   B   0.5   C   0.4   D   0.6   E   0.25

12. The table shows the amount of a cake eaten by four people. Who ate ³⁄₁₀ of the cake?

    Answer: _____

| Name | Amount of cake eaten |
|---|---|
| Kelly | 0.1 |
| Bethan | 0.35 |
| Susan | 0.3 |
| Gurpreet | 0.25 |

13. How many quarters are there in 0.75?

    Answer: _____

/ 5

Section One — Number Knowledge

# Section Two — Working with Numbers

## Addition

Write down the answer to each calculation.

1. 33 + 9        Answer: _____
2. 23 + 47       Answer: _____
3. 85 + 16       Answer: _____
4. 65 + 48       Answer: _____

 / 4

Write down the answer to each calculation.

5. 211 + 54      Answer: _____
6. 38 + 340      Answer: _____
7. 685 + 19      Answer: _____
8. 507 + 182     Answer: _____

 / 4

What is the total cost of buying the following items?

|  |  |
|---|---|
| Hat | £2.20 |
| Scarf | £7.40 |
| Shirt | £12.30 |
| Jumper | £15.50 |
| Jacket | £22.50 |

9. A jacket and a hat.          Answer: £ _____
10. A scarf and a jumper.       Answer: £ _____
11. A scarf and a jacket.       Answer: £ _____
12. A shirt and a scarf.        Answer: £ _____
13. A jumper and a shirt.       Answer: £ _____

/ 5

14. Mel has 45 tulips in her front garden and 46 tulips in her back garden. How many tulips does Mel have in total?

    Answer: _____

15. Mr Black grows two melons weighing 320 g and 446 g. How much do they weigh altogether?

    Answer: _____ g

16. Jane buys garden ornaments weighing 315 g and 350 g. What is their total weight?

    Answer: _____ g

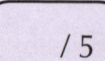 / 3

# Addition

17. Two planks of wood that measure 133 cm and 327 cm are laid end to end. What is the total length of the planks?   Answer: _____ cm

18. What is 199 + 178?   Answer: _____

19. What is the total of all of the numbers on this spinner?

    Answer: _____

20. 191 parents and 216 children went to a school concert. How many people went to the concert in total?

    Answer: _____

21. Which of these additions equals 90?  Circle the correct answer.

    A   71 + 21    C   57 + 33    E   43 + 37
    B   45 + 55    D   24 + 56

22. John ran two races in 152 seconds and 147 seconds. What was his total time for both races?

    Answer: _____ s

23. 336 Barchester City fans and 582 Dartfield fans were at a football match. How many fans were there altogether?  Circle the correct answer.

    A   958    B   918    C   988    D   888    E   998

24. Jake had fish and chips at the café. How much did he spend?

    Answer: £ _____

    Café Menu
    Chicken    £3.59
    Fish       £2.46
    Chips      £1.25
    Peas       45p
    Beans      35p

25. Add together 25, 85, 54 and 58.

    Answer: _____

/9

# Subtraction

Write down the answer to each calculation.

1. 73 – 12     Answer: _____
2. 69 – 34     Answer: _____
3. 100 – 47    Answer: _____
4. 125 – 77    Answer: _____

/ 4

Use each of the numbers in the box once to complete the calculations below.

| 87 | 126 | 49 | 24 | 121 |

5. 198 – 72 = _____
6. 249 – 225 = _____
7. 123 – _____ = 36
8. 166 – _____ = 45
9. 71 – _____ = 22

*Hint: For questions 7-9, you need to subtract the result of the calculation from the number you've been given.*

/ 5

10. John spends 78p. How much change will he get from £1?

    Answer: _____ p

11. Alisha spends £3.50. How much change will she get from £5?

    Answer: £ _____

12. Kate spends £2.60. How much change will she get from £5?

    Answer: £ _____

13. Sita spends £4.30. How much change will she get from £10?

    Answer: £ _____

14. Perry spends £7.85. How much change will he get from £10?

    Answer: £ _____

/ 5

# Subtraction

15. There were 132 people in a theatre. 16 people left during the interval. How many people were left in the theatre?

    Answer: _____

16. Which two numbers have a difference of 23? Circle the correct answer.

    **A** 32 and 15  **C** 67 and 24  **E** 43 and 25
    **B** 56 and 39  **D** 71 and 48

17. A pond was filled with 167 litres of water but 45 litres leaked out. How much water was left in the pond?

    Answer: _____ l

18. Mr Farr has a 300 cm piece of wood. He saws off 172 cm. What is the length of the remaining piece?

    Answer: _____ cm

19. 98 men and 265 women visited the local gym. How many more women went to the gym than men?

    Answer: _____

20. Terri has 387 points on a computer game but she loses 136 points. What is her final score? Circle the correct answer.

    **A** 523  **B** 251  **C** 257  **D** 243  **E** 351

21. Mr Samson enters three sunflowers in the local flower show. They are 178 cm, 213 cm and 163 cm tall. What is the difference in height between the shortest sunflower and the tallest sunflower? Circle the correct answer.

    **A** 350 cm  **B** 165 cm  **C** 50 cm  **D** 43 cm  **E** 52 cm

22. Patrick wants to buy a game costing £10.00. He has saved £6.65. How much more money does he need to save? Circle the correct answer.

    **A** £3.45  **B** £4.45  **C** £6.15  **D** £3.35  **E** £2.55

23. 317 − 38 = ☐

    Circle the missing number in this calculation.

    **A** 387  **B** 279  **C** 287  **D** 289  **E** 278

# Multiplying and Dividing by 10 and 100

Fill in the gaps to complete the calculations below.

1. 70 × 10 = _____

2. 62 × 10 = _____

3. 28 × 100 = _____

4. 510 ÷ 10 = _____

5. 6000 ÷ 100 = _____

/ 5

6. Farmer Joe's chickens lay 15 eggs every day. How many eggs will they have laid after 10 days?

   Answer: _____

7. Crisps cost 72p per packet. There are 10 packets in every box. What is the price of each box? Give your answer in pence.

   Answer: _____ p

8. Tickets for a school concert cost £10. The school sold £6210 worth of tickets. How many tickets were sold? Circle the correct answer.

   A   6210        B   621        C   62100        D   6.21        E   62

9. Jake has a plank of wood that is 500 cm long. He cuts the plank of wood into 10 equal pieces. How many centimetres long is each piece? Circle the correct answer.

   A   500 cm     B   0.5 cm     C   5 cm     D   50 cm     E   5000 cm

10. ☐ ÷ 10 = 44

    Circle the missing number in this calculation.

    A   44        B   4        C   4400        D   440        E   140

/ 5

Section Two — Working with Numbers

# Multiplication

The cost of some items in a shop are shown below.

Book £5    CD £7    Teddy Bear £6    Football £4

Work out how much each person spends.

1. Mabel buys 5 books.           Answer: £ _____
2. Mohammed buys 4 CDs.          Answer: £ _____
3. Phillip buys 6 teddy bears.   Answer: £ _____
4. Naomi buys 8 footballs.       Answer: £ _____
5. Bryony buys 9 CDs.            Answer: £ _____

/ 5

Write down the answer to each calculation.

6. 30 × 4    Answer: _____
7. 90 × 5    Answer: _____
8. 6 × 70    Answer: _____
9. 60 × 3    Answer: _____
10. 80 × 5   Answer: _____

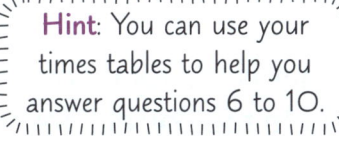

Hint: You can use your times tables to help you answer questions 6 to 10.

/ 5

Write down the answer to each calculation.

11. 15 × 6   Answer: _____
12. 27 × 3   Answer: _____
13. 43 × 5   Answer: _____
14. 36 × 4   Answer: _____
15. 5 × 45   Answer: _____

/ 5

Section Two — Working with Numbers

# Multiplication

16. ☐ × 9 = 36
    What is the missing number in this calculation?   Answer: _____

17. Ross buys eight packs of stickers. Each pack contains six stickers. How many stickers does he buy in total?
    Answer: _____

18. Mrs Robinson has a roll of ribbon. She cuts it into seven parts that are 5 m long each. How long was the roll of ribbon?   Answer: _____ m

19. A teacher marks 30 test papers. There are nine questions on each paper. How many questions does she mark in total?   Answer: _____

20. Which of the following calculations is correct? Circle the correct answer.
    A   6 × 7 = 42        C   6 × 9 = 63        E   7 × 7 = 48
    B   9 × 8 = 56        D   9 × 5 = 50

21. What is the total cost of three DVDs that cost 99p each? Circle the correct answer.
    A   £3.00     B   £3.03     C   £2.97     D   £2.91     E   £3.09

22. A hospital orders 30 boxes of bandages. Each box contains seven bandages. How many bandages does the hospital order? Circle the correct answer.
    A   210     B   140     C   224     D   196     E   188

23. A postman drives 8 kilometres each day. He works for 23 days each month. How many kilometres does the postman drive each month?
    Answer: _____ km

24. One coach can seat 33 people. How many people can four coaches seat? Circle the correct answer.
    A   106     B   132     C   124     D   120     E   99

/9

# Division

Write down the answer to each calculation.

1. 16 ÷ 2    Answer: _____
2. 27 ÷ 3    Answer: _____
3. 42 ÷ 6    Answer: _____
4. 36 ÷ 6    Answer: _____
5. 81 ÷ 9    Answer: _____

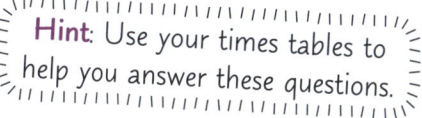

Hint: Use your times tables to help you answer these questions.

/ 5

Write down the remainder in each calculation.

6. 19 ÷ 2    Answer: _____
7. 46 ÷ 6    Answer: _____
8. 69 ÷ 9    Answer: _____
9. 68 ÷ 5    Answer: _____
10. 88 ÷ 7   Answer: _____

/ 5

Work out how much money each person will get.

11. £16 divided between 4 people.    Answer: £ _____
12. £75 divided between 5 people.    Answer: £ _____
13. £96 divided between 6 people.    Answer: £ _____
14. £128 divided between 4 people.   Answer: £ _____
15. £57 divided between 3 people.    Answer: £ _____

/ 5

Section Two — Working with Numbers

# Division

16. A bookshelf has three shelves. Jim divides 69 books equally between the three shelves. How many books are there on each shelf?    Answer: _____

17. A box of 96 chocolates is divided equally between eight friends. How many chocolates does each friend get? Circle the correct answer.

    **A** 15     **B** 12     **C** 9     **D** 11     **E** 13

18. Farmer Giles has 86 eggs. He packs them into boxes of 6. How many eggs does he have left over?

    Answer: _____

19. Look at the calculations given below. Circle the calculation that is incorrect.

    **A**  125 ÷ 5 = 25       **C**  58 ÷ 7 = 8        **E**  121 ÷ 11 = 11
    **B**  72 ÷ 6 = 12        **D**  350 ÷ 5 = 70

20. Which of these numbers can be exactly divided by four? Circle the correct answer.

    **A** 50     **B** 87     **C** 58     **D** 60     **E** 73

21. 68 ÷ 9 = ☐ remainder 5

    What is the missing number in this calculation?    Answer: _____

22. Phoebe has 79 coins in her coin collection. She places all of the coins in an album. Each page of the album holds seven coins. How many pages will she need to fit all 79 coins in her album?    Answer: _____

23. June has 39 brownies. She divides all of the brownies equally between four boxes but she has some left over. How many brownies does she have left over? Circle the correct answer.

    **A** 1     **B** 2     **C** 3     **D** 4     **E** 5

# Section Three — Word Problems

## Word Problems

1. Beth spent £2.50 on two mugs of hot chocolate and one banana milkshake. The banana milkshake cost 50p. How much did each mug of hot chocolate cost?

   Answer: £ _____

2. Mr Warren brought 10 boxes of fizzy sweets to a school party. Each box contained 128 fizzy sweets. How many fizzy sweets did Mr Warren bring in total?

   Answer: _____

3. Darren bought 4 chews and 1 chocolate mouse from the tuck shop. How much did Darren pay?

   Answer: _____ p

   | Tuck Shop Prices | |
   | --- | --- |
   | Chews | 8p each |
   | Lollies | 10p each |
   | Chocolate mice | 12p each |
   | Jelly worms | 6p each |

4. Waleed paid £20 for six cinema tickets. He received £2 in change. How much did each cinema ticket cost?

   Answer: £ _____

5. Jodie wants to buy a jacket that costs £40, but she only has £20. She saves £4 each week until she has enough money to buy the jacket. How many weeks did she need to save for? Circle the correct answer.

   A  5    B  10    C  7    D  4    E  8

6. Callum thinks of a number. He divides it by 4 and ends up with 6. What number did Callum start with? Circle the correct answer.

   A  24    B  18    C  15    D  1.5    E  12

7. William has £10 to spend on his mum's birthday presents. Which of the following would cost exactly £10? Circle the correct answer.

   A  2 scarves and 1 plant.
   B  2 bottles of perfume.
   C  1 bottle of perfume and 2 scarves.
   D  2 plants and 1 scarf.
   E  1 plant and 1 bottle of perfume.

   Plant £5
   Perfume £7
   Scarf £1.50

8. Nicola's dad is exactly 6 times as old as she is. Which of these is her dad's age? Circle the correct answer.

   A  32    B  36    C  41    D  28    E  38

/ 8

# Word Problems

9. Mr Bracken paid £15 for 10 litres of petrol for his car. He used 6 litres of petrol to drive to his aunt's house. How much did the petrol for this journey cost?

   Answer: £ _____

10. Robin multiplies 3 by 8 and divides the answer by 6. Arjen also starts with 3, but does a different calculation. Both boys get the same answer. Which of these calculations could Arjen have done? Circle the correct answer.

    A   Multiply a number by 4 then divide by 3.
    B   Multiply a number by 16 then divide by 2.
    C   Multiply a number by 4 then divide by 2.
    D   Multiply a number by 2 then divide by 4.
    E   Multiply a number by 2 then divide by 3.

11. Mrs Price is making costumes for a play. She can make 3 rabbit costumes and 2 squirrel costumes from 5 metres of fabric. How many metres of fabric will she need to make 9 rabbit costumes and 6 squirrel costumes?

    Answer: _____ m

12. The table shows the ingredients used to make pasta carbonara for 4 people. How much pasta would be needed for exactly 5 people?

    Answer: _____ g

    | Pasta Carbonara (serves 4) | |
    |---|---|
    | Pasta | 400 g |
    | Cream | 100 ml |
    | Ham | 100 g |
    | Shallots | 2 |

13. Yolanda pays for 6 books using two £15 book tokens. The books are all the same price and she gets no change. How much does each book cost?

    Answer: £ _____

14. A pack of butter weighs 200 g and is 4 cm tall. Penny places packs of butter on top of each other to make a stack that is 12 cm tall. What is the weight of the stack of butter? Circle the correct answer.

    A   800 g        C   12 g        E   48 g
    B   200 g        D   600 g

    Hint: Start by working out the number of packs of butter in the stack.

15. Hair clips cost £1.50 each. How many hair clips can Martha afford to buy with £10?

    Answer: _____

# Section Four — Data Handling

## Data Tables

Look at the school uniform order form.
Use the form to answer these questions.

| School Uniform Order Form | | |
|---|---|---|
| Item | Price (each) | Number Ordered |
| Shirt | £5.99 | 3 |
| Trousers | £10.99 | 1 |
| Jumper | £12.99 | 1 |
| Shorts | £5.99 | 2 |
| Blazer | £19.99 | 1 |

1. How many shirts have been ordered?

    Answer: _____

2. Which item costs £12.99?

    Answer: _____

3. What is the most expensive item of uniform?

    Answer: _____

4. Which item has been ordered twice?    Answer: _____

5. How many items have been ordered in total?    Answer: _____

/ 5

6. The table shows the number of pets owned by the children in Class D.

    | Number of pets owned | 1 | 2 | 3 | 4 | 5 |
    |---|---|---|---|---|---|
    | Number of children | 7 | 8 | 3 | 4 | 3 |

    How many children own two pets?    Answer: _____

7. The table shows information about four towns. Which two towns have the same number of shops and the same number of parks?
Circle the correct answer.

    A   Dellville and Coalton
    B   Herdnell and Dellville
    C   Coalton and Nolanbeck
    D   Dellville and Nolanbeck
    E   Herdnell and Nolanbeck

    | Town | Population | Number of shops | Number of parks |
    |---|---|---|---|
    | Herdnell | 16 500 | 112 | 4 |
    | Dellville | 28 000 | 136 | 6 |
    | Coalton | 35 500 | 207 | 6 |
    | Nolanbeck | 28 000 | 112 | 4 |

8. The table shows the number of boys and girls in Years 4 and 5 at Westfield School. What is the total number of children in Year 5?

    | | Girls | Boys | Total |
    |---|---|---|---|
    | Year 4 | 13 | 12 | 25 |
    | Year 5 | 17 | 14 | ? |

    Answer: _____

/ 3

# Data Tables

9. The table shows the temperature of the water in Tony's bath over a 3 hour period. Between which two times did the temperature fall by 5 °C? Circle the correct answer.

   A  12:00 and 12:30    D  14:00 and 14:30

   B  12:30 and 13:00    E  14:30 and 15:00

   C  13:00 and 13:30

| Time | Temperature (°C) |
|---|---|
| 12:00 | 42 |
| 12:30 | 39 |
| 13:00 | 34 |
| 13:30 | 30 |
| 14:00 | 28 |
| 14:30 | 25 |
| 15:00 | 21 |

10. 40 children were asked how they travel to school. The results are shown in the table. How many children did not travel to school by car? Circle the correct answer.

|  | Car | Bus | Bike | Train | Walk |
|---|---|---|---|---|---|
| Number of children | 8 | 3 | 6 | 2 | 21 |

   A  26    B  32    C  19    D  8    E  22

11. Mrs Chung is putting her shopping bill into this table. How many onions did she buy?

    Answer: _____

| Item | Number Bought | Cost (per item) | Total Cost |
|---|---|---|---|
| Cereal | 2 | £2.60 | £5.20 |
| Milk | 1 | £1.90 | £1.90 |
| Baked Beans | 4 | 70p | £2.80 |
| Onions | ? | 20p | £1.40 |

| Marks | Boys | Girls |
|---|---|---|
| 0 – 20 | 2 | 1 |
| 21 – 40 | 3 | 4 |
| 41 – 60 | 2 | 8 |
| 61 – 80 | 10 | ? |
| 81 – 100 | 3 | 2 |

12. 20 boys and 20 girls did a maths test. Some of their marks are shown in the table. How many girls scored 61-80 marks?

    Answer: _____

| Item | Number sold | | |
|---|---|---|---|
|  | Morning | Afternoon | Total |
| Doughnuts |  | 10 | 26 |
| Cookies | 7 | 11 | 18 |
| Brownies | ? | 24 |  |

13. A bakery started to record the number of items it sold in one day in this table. They sold 30 items altogether in the morning. How many brownies did they sell in the morning?

    Answer: _____

Hint: Start by working out the number of doughnuts sold in the morning.

# Displaying Data

Mr Potter made this bar chart to show how many tomatoes he picked each day. Use the bar chart to answer questions 1-4.

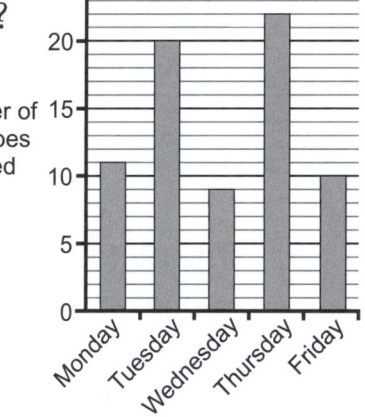

1. On which day did Mr Potter pick the most tomatoes?

    Answer: _____

2. On which day were 10 tomatoes picked?

    Answer: _____

3. How many tomatoes were picked on Monday?

    Answer: _____

4. What was the total number of tomatoes picked on Thursday and Friday?

    Answer: _____

/ 4

5. Shirley made this pictogram to show the different buttons that she found in her drawer.
   How many red buttons did she find? Circle the correct answer.

   | Button colour | Number of buttons |
   |---|---|
   | White | ⊙ ⊙ ⊙ ⊙ ⊙ |
   | Red | ⊙ ⊙ ☽ |
   | Black | ⊙ ⊙ ⊙ ⊙ |

   ⊙ = 4 buttons

   A  2.5     D  3
   B  12      E  10
   C  4

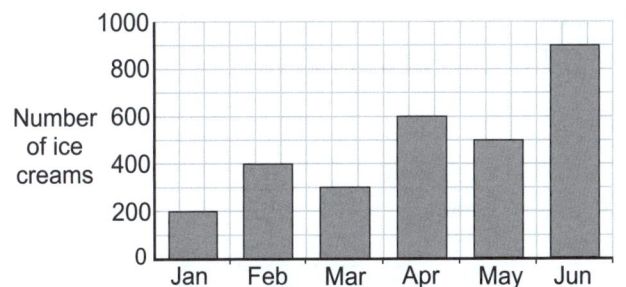

6. The bar chart shows the number of ice creams sold from an ice cream van over six months. In which month were 300 ice creams sold?

    Answer: _____

7. Alexa counted the number of chickens, ducks and turkeys she saw at a farm. The pictogram shows her results. How many more ducks did she see than turkeys?

    Answer: _____

   | Chickens | 🥚🥚🥚🥚 |
   |---|---|
   | Ducks | 🥚🥚🥚 |
   | Turkeys | 🥚◗ |

   🥚 = 6 birds

/ 3

Section Four — Data Handling

# Displaying Data

8. Jeremy made this chart to show the amount of piano practice he did each day. How many minutes of practice did he do in total?

    Answer: _____ minutes

    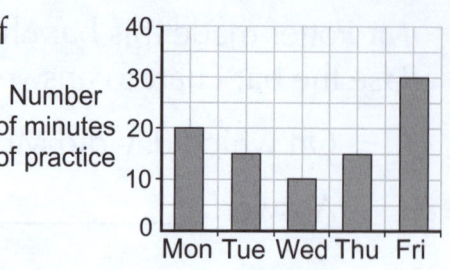

9. The pictogram shows the number of goals scored by Milton United in their matches. In how many matches did they score 2 or more goals?

    Answer: _____

    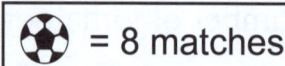

10. The bar chart shows the amount of sport played each week by a group of children. Which of the following sentences is true? Circle the correct answer.

    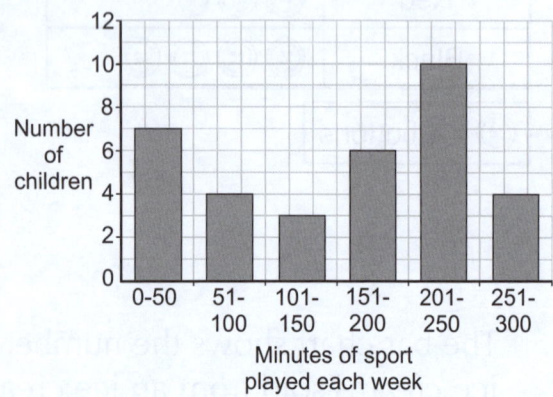

    A  5 children play 251-300 minutes of sport.

    B  8 children play less than 50 minutes of sport.

    C  Most of the children play 101-150 minutes of sport.

    D  4 children play 251-300 minutes of sport.

    E  An even number of children play 0-50 minutes of sport.

11. 26 people voted for their favourite crisp flavour. Hans made a bar chart to show the results, but forgot to fill in the bar for prawn cocktail flavour. How many people voted for prawn cocktail?

    Answer: _____

    Hint: Start by working out the total number of people who voted for the other three flavours.

/ 4

Section Four — Data Handling

# Section Five — Shape and Space

## Angles

Look at the angles below and answer questions 1-4.

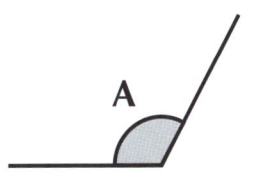 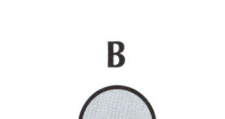 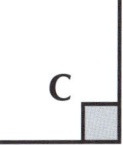 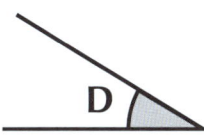

A     B     C     D

1. Which angle is exactly 90°?    Answer: _____
2. Which angle is smaller than 90°?    Answer: _____
3. Which angle is exactly 180°?    Answer: _____
4. Which angle is between 90° and 180°?    Answer: _____

/ 4

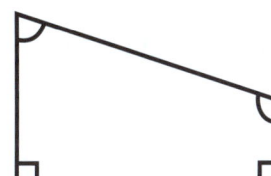

5. How many right angles are there in this shape? Circle the correct answer.

    **A**   0    **B**   1    **C**   2    **D**   3    **E**   4

6. The hour hand on this clock is pointing at 12. What number will the hour hand be pointing at if it turns 90° clockwise?

Answer: _____

7. Circle the smallest angle.

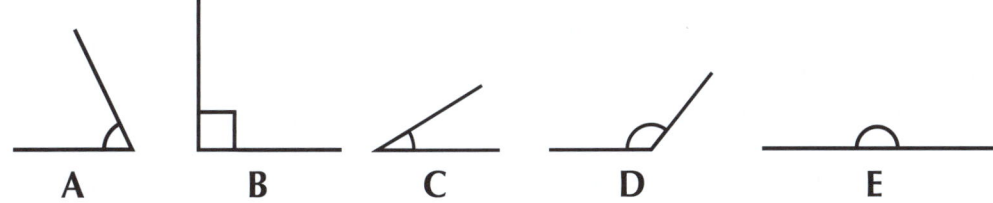

   A      B      C      D      E

8. Josie is facing south. She turns clockwise to face north. How many right angles has she turned through?

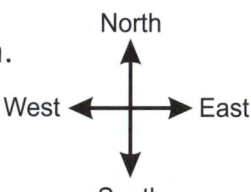

Answer: _____

9. Estimate the size of angle *a*. Circle the correct answer.

    100°     45°     180°     90°     125°   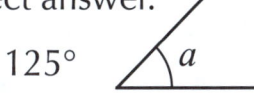

/ 5

# 2D Shapes

Match each shape below to its description.

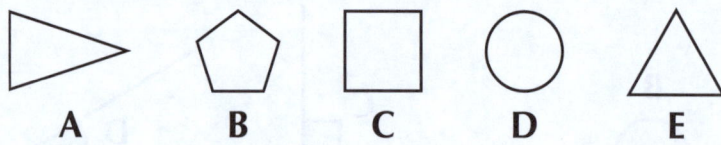

1. It is a shape with five sides and five corners. Answer: _____
2. It is a shape with no corners. Answer: _____
3. It has three equal sides and three equal angles. Answer: _____
4. It is a triangle with only two equal sides. Answer: _____
5. It has four equal sides and four right angles. Answer: _____

/ 5

6. Which of these shapes is an equilateral triangle? Circle the correct answer.

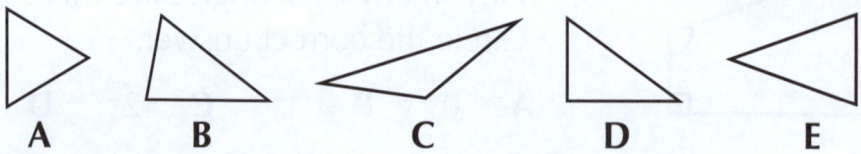

7. Which of these shapes is not a quadrilateral? Circle the correct answer.

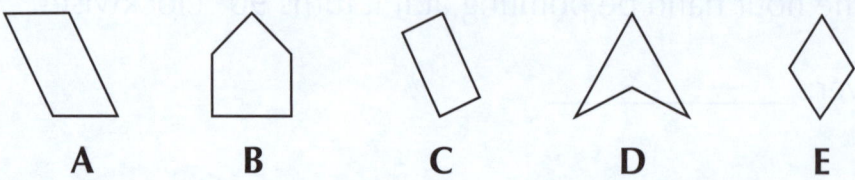

8. Which of these shapes should be placed into the shaded box of the sorting table? Circle the correct answer.

   **A** regular pentagon    **D** regular octagon
   **B** regular hexagon    **E** square
   **C** equilateral triangle

   |  | At least 1 right angle | It does not have right angles |
   |---|---|---|
   | All sides are equal in length |  |  |
   | Not all sides are equal in length |  |  |

9. Which of these shapes does not have any equal angles? Circle the correct answer.

 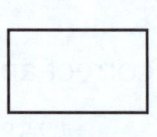   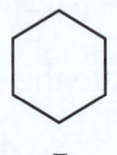
   A         B         C         D         E

/ 4

Section Five — Shape and Space

# 2D Shapes — Area and Perimeter

Indira drew some shapes on squared paper. The area of each square on the paper is 1 cm².

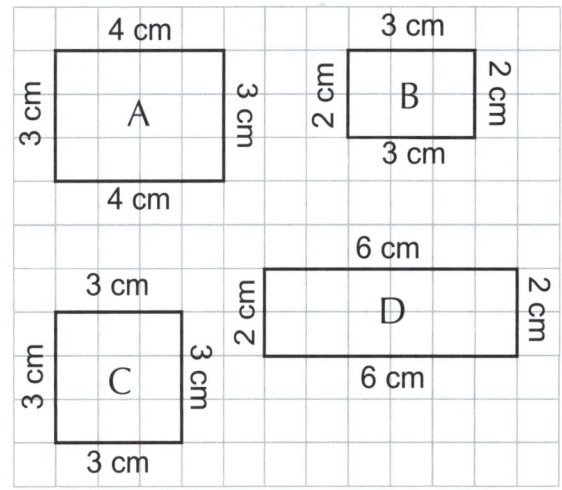

1. What is the perimeter of shape C?

   Answer: _____ cm

2. Which shape has a perimeter of 10 cm?

   Answer: _____

3. What is the area of shape D?

   Answer: _____ cm²

4. What is the area of shape C?  Answer: _____ cm²

5. What is the perimeter of shape A?  Answer: _____ cm

/ 5

6. A hexagon has six sides that are each 4 cm long. What is the perimeter of the hexagon?

   Answer: _____ cm

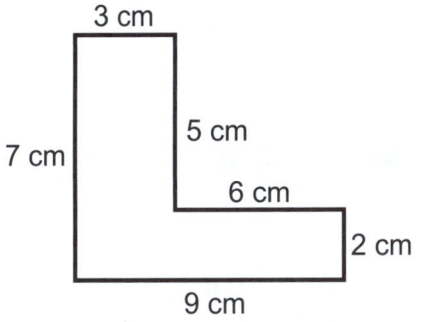

7. What is the perimeter of this shape? Circle the correct answer.

   A  30 cm     C  31 cm     E  29 cm
   B  28 cm     D  32 cm

8. Each square on this diagram has an area of 1 cm². What is the area of the triangle?

   Answer: _____ cm²

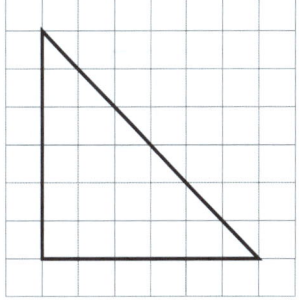

9. Mr Stiles has a rectangular vegetable patch with a perimeter of 28 m. The two longest sides are both 10 m long. What is the width of the vegetable patch? Circle the correct answer.

   A  8 m       C  3 m       E  4 m
   B  5 m       D  10 m

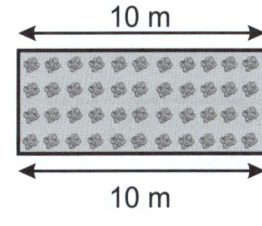

/ 4

Section Five — Shape and Space

# Symmetry

Look at the shapes below and answer questions 1-5.

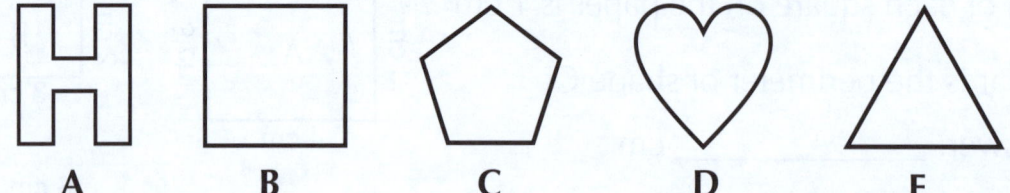

1. Which shape has four lines of symmetry? Answer: _____

2. Which shape has one line of symmetry? Answer: _____

3. Which shape has three lines of symmetry? Answer: _____

4. Which shape has two lines of symmetry? Answer: _____

5. Which shape has five lines of symmetry? Answer: _____   / 5

6. How many lines of symmetry does this rectangle have?

   Answer: _____

7. Which of the following letters has no lines of symmetry? Circle the correct answer.

   **M   T   D   V   N**

8. The shape on the right is reflected in the vertical mirror line. Circle the option which shows the reflection of the shape.

   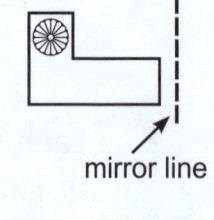

   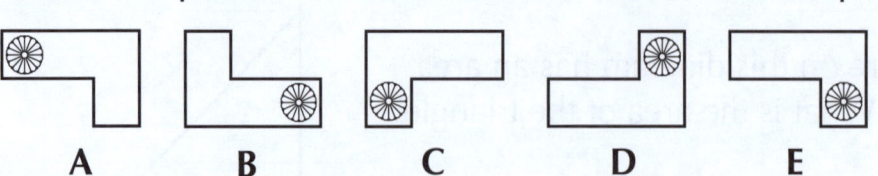
   A      B      C      D      E

   mirror line

9. Point X is reflected in the horizontal mirror line. Which letter shows the position of its reflection? Circle the correct answer.

   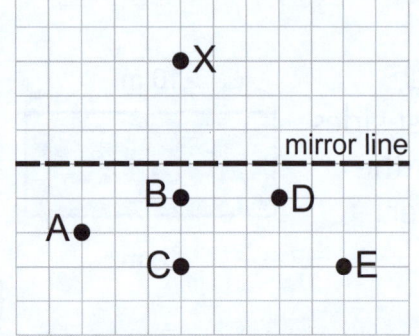

   A   B   C   D   E

   / 4

Section Five — Shape and Space

# 3D Shapes

Match each 3D shape below to its description.

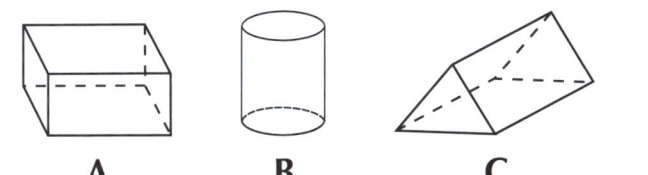

1. A shape with 3 faces. Answer: _____

2. A shape with 6 faces and 12 edges. Answer: _____

3. A shape with 4 faces and 6 edges. Answer: _____

4. A shape with 5 faces and 9 edges. Answer: _____

5. A shape with 5 faces and 8 edges. Answer: _____

/ 5

6. Jack is making a gift box. He uses this net. Which 3D shape does Jack make? Circle the correct answer.

   A pyramid    C cube    E sphere
   B cone    D cylinder

7. Ravi picks a 3D shape at random. It has 7 faces. Which of the following could be Ravi's shape? Circle the correct answer.

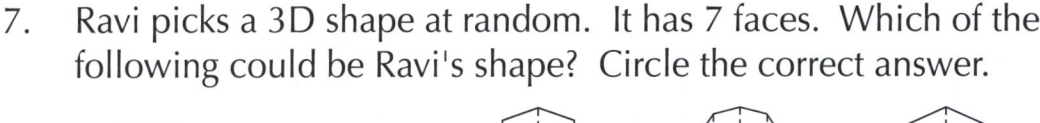

8. Rebecca made a 3D shape from this net. What shape did she make? Circle the correct answer.

   A cube    D triangle-based pyramid
   B quadrilateral    E hexagonal prism
   C triangular prism

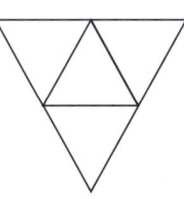

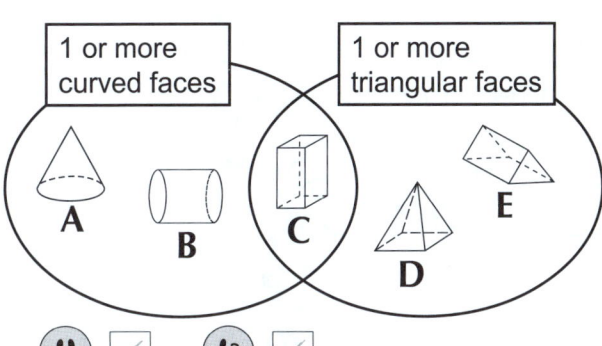

9. Which shape should not be in the Venn diagram? Circle the correct answer.

   A    B    C    D    E

/ 4

Section Five — Shape and Space

# Shape Problems

Look at the shapes below and answer questions 1-5.

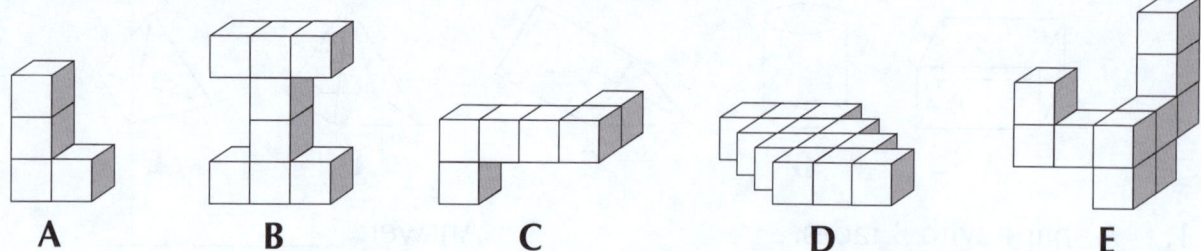

1. Which shape contains 4 cubes?    Answer: _____
2. Which shape contains 6 cubes?    Answer: _____
3. Which shape contains 8 cubes?    Answer: _____
4. Which shape contains 10 cubes?   Answer: _____
5. Which shape contains 12 cubes?   Answer: _____

/ 5

6. Chris fits two smaller shapes together to make shape X. Which two shapes did he use? Circle the correct answer.

   Hint: You may have to reflect one of the shapes.

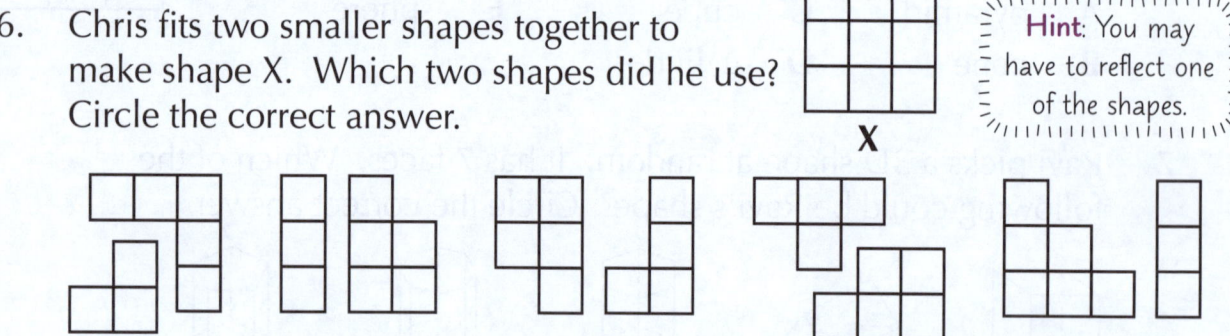

7. Dominic reflects the shape on the right in the mirror line. Which of the following shows the reflected shape? Circle the correct answer.

   mirror line

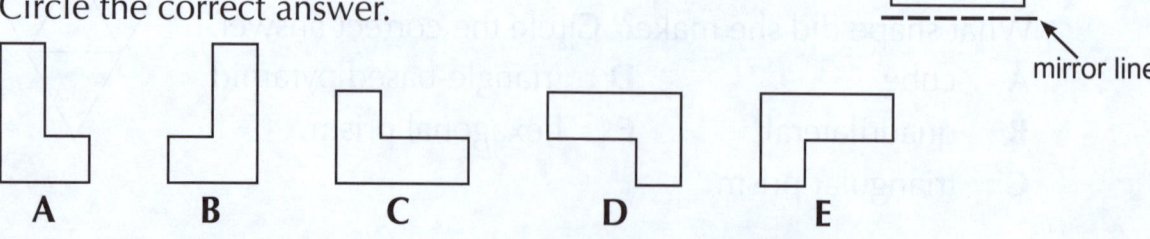

8. Which of these shapes is exactly the same shape as shape W? Circle the correct answer.

/ 3

Section Five — Shape and Space

# Coordinates

Sasha drew some objects on a coordinate grid. Write down the coordinates of these objects:

1. the book.   Answer: _____
2. the tent.   Answer: _____
3. the bear.   Answer: _____
4. the church. Answer: _____
5. the car.    Answer: _____

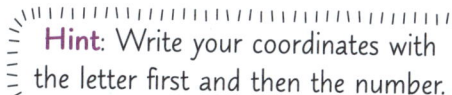

Hint: Write your coordinates with the letter first and then the number.

/ 5

6. Carlos is drawing shapes on a coordinate grid. What shape has he drawn in the square B3? Circle the correct answer.

   A  circle    D  hexagon
   B  star      E  triangle
   C  square

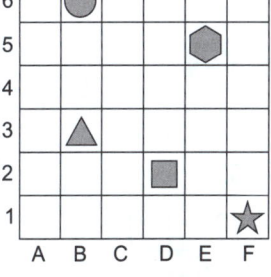

7. The coordinates of point A are (1, 2). What are the coordinates of point B? Circle the correct answer.

   A  (3, 7)    D  (7, 4)
   B  (5, 9)    E  (2, 6)
   C  (3, 9)

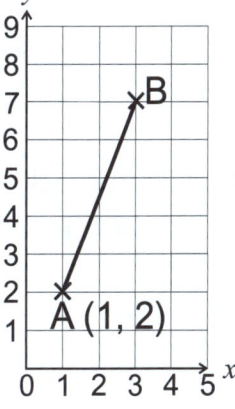

Hint: When you're writing coordinates, put the *x*-axis coordinate first and then the *y*-axis coordinate.

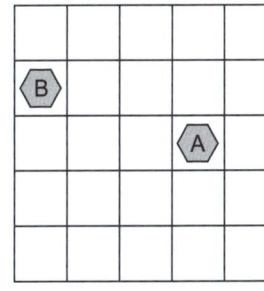

8. Shape B on the grid is a translation of shape A. Which of the following describes the translation? Circle the correct answer.

   A  three squares right, two squares up
   B  two squares left, one square up
   C  three squares left, one square up
   D  three squares left, one square down
   E  two squares right, two squares down

/ 3

Section Five — Shape and Space

# Section Six — Units and Measures

## Units

Look at these measurements.

| 100 m | 100 g | 0.3 litres | 5 ml | 7 cm |

Choose the most likely measurement for each of the following.

1. The volume of liquid in a full mug of tea.   Answer: _____

2. The length of a finger.   Answer: _____

3. The weight of a mobile phone.   Answer: _____

4. The volume of medicine in a teaspoonful.   Answer: _____

5. The length of a football pitch.   Answer: _____

/ 5

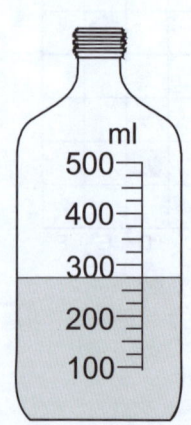

6. How much liquid is in the bottle on the left?

    Answer: _____ ml

7. Mrs Patel bought 30 cm of gold chain and 1.5 m of silver chain. How many centimetres of chain did she buy altogether?

    Answer: _____ cm

8. Lucas has some 500 ml bottles of cola. He pours them into a 2 litre jug. How many bottles are needed to fill the jug?

    Answer: _____

9. A baker fills 10 bags with doughnuts. Each bag of doughnuts weighs 350 g. What is the total weight of all the bags? Circle the correct answer.

    A   3.5 kg       B   35 kg       C   350 kg       D   35 g       E   3.5 g

10. Deepak is doing a 10 km run. He has run $9\frac{3}{4}$ km. How many more metres are left to run? Circle the correct answer.

    A   $\frac{1}{4}$ m       B   25 m       C   250 m       D   750 m       E   300 m

/ 5

# Time

| 4:50 | 5:45 | 5:10 | 7:30 | 6:15 |
|------|------|------|------|------|
| A | B | C | D | E |

Write the letter of the time above that is the same as:

1. Ten minutes to five. Answer: _____

2. Half past seven. Answer: _____

3. Quarter to six. Answer: _____

4. Half an hour earlier than qua[rter past seven]. Answer: _____

5. Twenty minutes later than ten minutes to five. Answer: _____ / 5

EM 21/3/23

6. This timetable shows the times of buses going from Whitdale to the Hospital. Sarah needs to be at the Hospital at 11:00. What is the latest time that she can catch the bus from Whitdale? Circle the correct answer.

   | Whitdale | 10:15 | 10:30 | 10:45 |
   |----------|-------|-------|-------|
   | Thornby  | 10:25 | 10:40 | 10:55 |
   | Hospital | 10:40 | 10:55 | 11:10 |

   A  10:15     B  10:30     C  10:45     D  10:40     E  10:55

7. Jo goes on holiday on Tuesday 24th May. The last day of her holiday is the 13th June. How many weeks was she on holiday for?

   Hint: Make sure you know how many days there are in each month.

   Answer: _____ weeks

8. Lokesh starts his homework at 6:45 pm. He finishes it 70 minutes later. What time does he finish his homework? Answer: ____:____ pm

9. Mrs Brown is going to a school concert. The concert starts at 3:15 pm. It takes her 35 minutes to drive to the school and 5 minutes to park her car and walk to the school. What time must she leave home? Answer: ____:____ pm

10. The time in Sydney, Australia, is 11 hours later than in the UK. When it is 10:15 am in the UK, what time is it in Sydney? Circle the correct answer.

    A  9:15 am     C  10:15 am     E  11:15 pm
    B  11:15 am    D  9:15 pm

/ 5

Section Six — Units and Measures

# Section Seven — Mixed Problems

# Mixed Problems

1. Which one of these shapes can be placed in the shaded area of the Venn diagram? Circle the correct answer.

   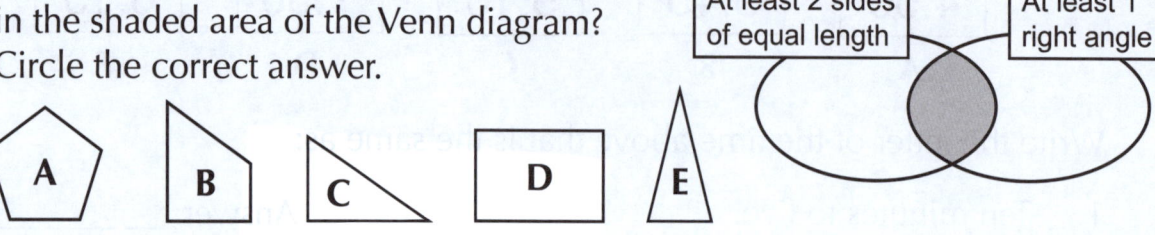

   At least 2 sides of equal length / At least 1 right angle

2. Anna worked for 4½ hours on Saturday and 5½ hours on Sunday. She is paid £4.50 for each hour of work. How much money did she earn in total?

   Hint: Start by working out the total number of hours that Anna worked.

   Answer: £ _____

3. A 500 ml bottle of water costs 40p. How much will it cost to buy 3 litres of water?

   Answer: £ _____

4. What fraction of these shapes have a line of symmetry? Circle the correct answer.

   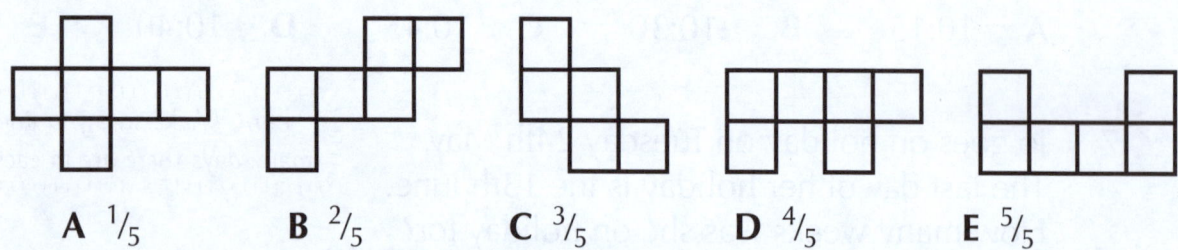

   A  1/5     B  2/5     C  3/5     D  4/5     E  5/5

5. Hilda starts washing eight cars at 4:45 pm. It takes her 10 minutes to wash each car. What time will she finish washing the cars? Circle the correct answer.

   A  5:45 pm     B  5:05 pm     C  6:30 pm     D  5:30 pm     E  6:05 pm

6. Lucy runs 8 km in an hour. How many metres does she run in 15 minutes?

   Answer: _____ m

7. Fran drew the shape on the right and reflected it in the mirror line. What is the total perimeter of the shape and its reflection? Circle the correct answer.

   A  24 cm     C  16 cm     E  20 cm
   B  28 cm     D  12 cm

   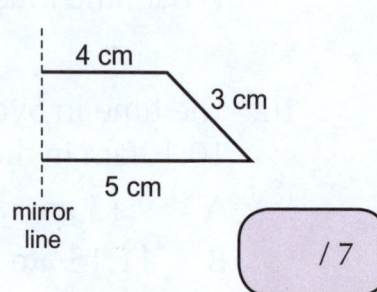

   /7

# Assessment Test 1

The rest of the book contains six assessment tests to help you improve your maths skills. Allow 35 minutes to do each test and work as quickly and as carefully as you can.

If you want to attempt each test more than once, you will need to print **multiple-choice answer sheets** for these questions from our website — go to cgpbooks.co.uk/11plus/answer-sheets or scan the QR code on the right. If you'd prefer to answer them in standard write-in format, either write your answers in the spaces provided or circle the **correct answer** from the options **A** to **E**.

1. Max has the following values of coins.
   How much money does he have?

   £2  £1  5p  2p  2p

   A  £3.90    D  £3.54
   B  £2.09    E  £2.90
   C  £3.09

2. Pat and Imran are at the Post Office.
   They walk 2 squares north and 1 square east.

   Where do they walk to?

   A  Leisure Centre
   B  Library
   C  Supermarket
   D  Newsagent
   E  Sports Shop

   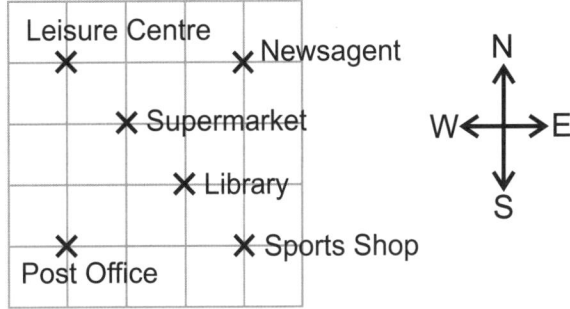

3. What is 295 rounded to the nearest 10?

   A  200   B  250   C  280   D  290   E  300

4. Hannah records the number of plants in her garden on a pictogram.

   How many bean plants does she have?

   A  3      C  4      E  1½
   B  5      D  2½

   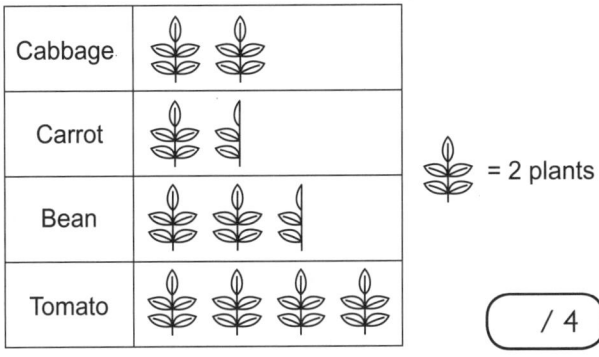

   / 4

   **Carry on to the next question → →**

   Assessment Test 1

5. How many lines of symmetry does a regular pentagon have?

   A 4   B 7   C 6   D 5   E 8

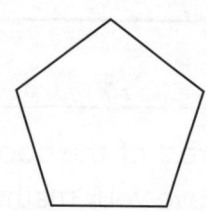

6. $7 \times 8 = 56$

   What is $7 \times 80$?

   A 73   B 490   C 650   D 560   E 87

7. This chart shows how many children go to different clubs.

   How many more children go to art club than to dance club?

   Answer: _____

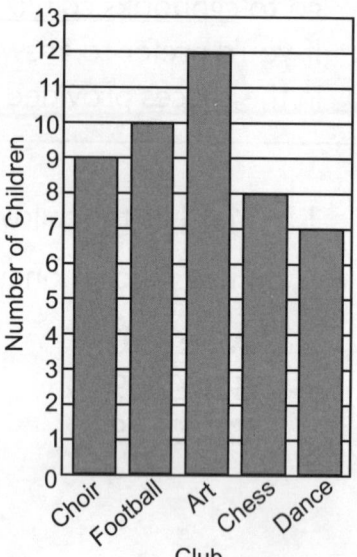

8. Which of the following pairs of numbers are factors of 36?

   A  4 and 8       C  7 and 12      E  6 and 7
   B  6 and 9       D  5 and 8

9. Which of these angles is bigger than 90°?

 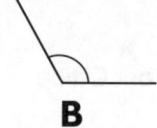   

   A            B            C            D            E

10. Which of these is the missing label from this Venn diagram?

    A  Multiples of 11
    B  Even numbers
    C  Odd numbers
    D  Multiples of 7
    E  Multiples of 6

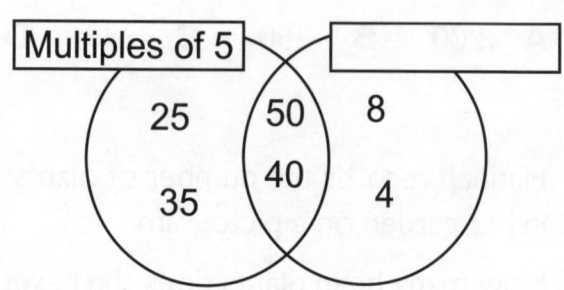

11. What is the difference between 998 and 1029?

    A 1971   B 31   C 32   D 28   E 2027

12. Julia buys some bags of biscuits for her dog.
    There are 8 biscuits in each bag.

    She gets 48 biscuits altogether. How many bags did she buy?

    Answer: _____

13. Each square in the shape on the right has an area of 1 cm². What is the area of the shape? 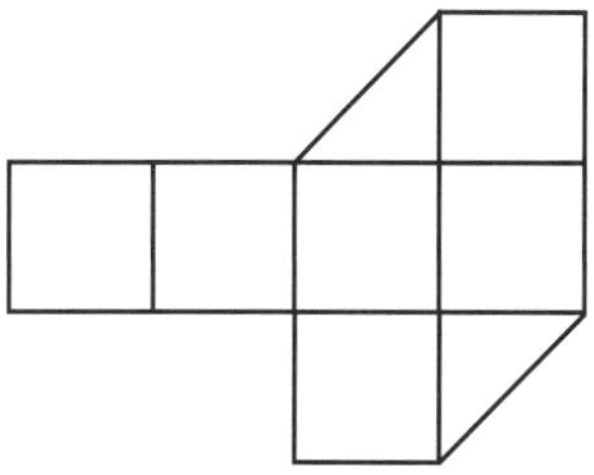
    - **A** 7 cm²
    - **B** 5½ cm²
    - **C** 5 cm²
    - **D** 6 cm²
    - **E** 8 cm²

14. Jill recorded the temperature on five mornings. She put her results in this table.

    Which morning was coldest?

    Answer: _____

    | Day | Temperature |
    |---|---|
    | Monday | 0 °C |
    | Tuesday | 2 °C |
    | Wednesday | −1 °C |
    | Thursday | −3 °C |
    | Friday | −2 °C |

15. What number is shown by the Roman numeral XXXIV?
    - **A** 36
    - **B** 24
    - **C** 33
    - **D** 34
    - **E** 26

16. What is 43 multiplied by 8?   Answer: _____

17. Look at the table on the right.

    How much carbohydrate and fat is there altogether in 100 g of bread?
    - **A** 58 g
    - **B** 49 g
    - **C** 52 g
    - **D** 36 g
    - **E** 51 g

    | In 100 g of bread there is: | |
    |---|---|
    | Protein | 9 g |
    | Carbohydrate | 49 g |
    | Fat | 2 g |
    | Fibre | 3 g |
    | Salt | 1 g |

18. Which of these shapes is irregular?

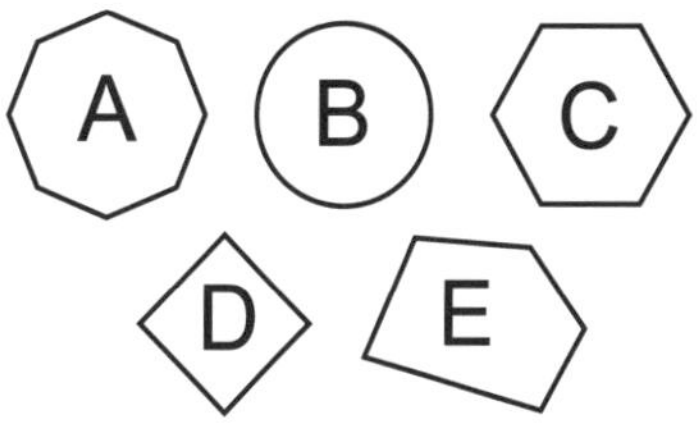

    Answer: _____

**Carry on to the next question → →**

Assessment Test 1

19. What number is the arrow pointing to on the number line?

    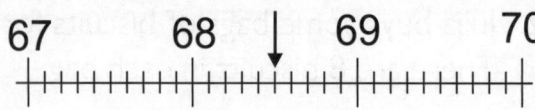

    A  69.5
    B  67.5
    C  68.5
    D  68.2
    E  68.9

20. John bought 10 identical stamps. They cost £3.60 altogether. How much did each stamp cost?

    Answer: _____ p

21. Which of these fractions is smallest?

    A  ¾    B  ½    C  ⅛    D  ¼    E  ⅜

22. This diagram shows the length and width of a school playground.

    What is the perimeter of the playground?

    Answer: _____ m

    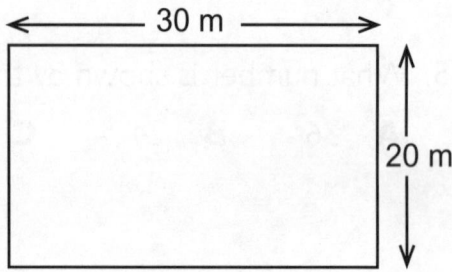

23. Jay receives £2.40 pocket money every week.

    How many weeks will it take him to save £7.20?

    Answer: _____ weeks

24. Tara thinks of a shape. It has 5 faces and 9 edges. Which of the following could be Tara's shape?

     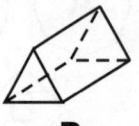  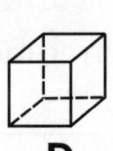 
    A           B           C           D           E

    / 6

25. 7 + 7 + 7 + 7 = ☐ × 2

    What is the missing number?

    **A** 7   **B** 14   **C** 28   **D** 11   **E** 17

26. Siti goes cycling at 1.30 pm. She spends 35 minutes cycling and then takes a 15 minute break.

    What time does her break finish?

    **A** 2:10 pm   **C** 2:15 am   **E** 2:20 am
    **B** 2:15 pm   **D** 2:20 pm

27. Claire has 80 stickers. She gives ½ of them to Luke. Luke then gives ¼ of his stickers to Jenny.

    How many stickers does Jenny get?

    **A** 40   **B** 30   **C** 20   **D** 10   **E** 5

28. Jemma makes a chart which shows the hair colour of the children in her class.

    Which of these sentences is not true?

    **A** 6 children have black hair.
    **B** Brown is the most common hair colour.
    **C** There are 28 children in Jemma's class.
    **D** 8 more children have brown hair than have blonde hair.
    **E** 15 children have brown or red hair.

    | Colour | Number of children |
    |---|---|
    | Brown | 14 |
    | Black | 6 |
    | Blonde | 7 |
    | Red | 1 |

29. Suki has a 2 m roll of ribbon. She cuts off 2 pieces of ribbon each measuring 75 cm.

    How much ribbon is left on the roll?

    **A** 1.25 m   **B** 0.75 m   **C** 50 m   **D** 5 m   **E** 0.5 m

30. Ruth thinks of a number. She multiplies it by 7 and then she adds 1. She ends up with 50.

    What number did she start with?

    **A** 5   **C** 6   **E** 9
    **B** 8   **D** 7

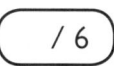

**End of Test**

# Assessment Test 2

Allow 35 minutes to do this test. Work as quickly and as carefully as you can.

You can print **multiple-choice answer sheets** for these questions from our website — go to cgpbooks.co.uk/11plus/answer-sheets or scan the QR code on the right. If you'd prefer to answer them in standard write-in format, either write your answers in the spaces provided or circle the **correct answer** from the options **A** to **E**.

1. What is the value of the 7 in 7052?
    - **A** seven tenths
    - **B** seventy thousand
    - **C** seven hundred
    - **D** seven thousand
    - **E** seventy

2. How many edges does a cube have?
    - **A** 12  **B** 6  **C** 7  **D** 8  **E** 9

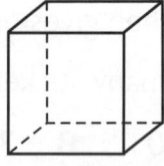

3. Which of the following numbers divides exactly by 8?
    - **A** 12  **B** 63  **C** 72  **D** 84  **E** 94

4. Ahmed asked the children in his class to name their favourite type of dog. He put the results in this bar chart.

    How many children chose the most popular type of dog?
    - **A** 9
    - **B** 10
    - **C** 11
    - **D** 12
    - **E** 37

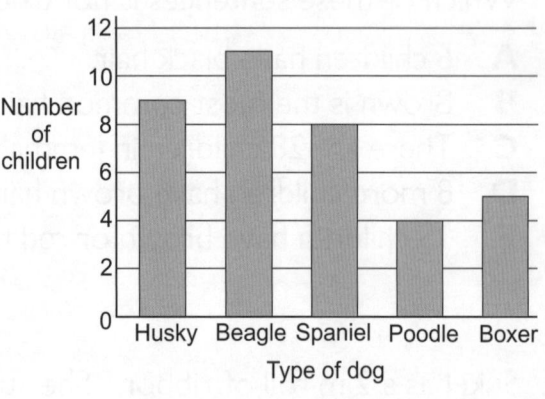

5. Look at these numbers.

    | 0.35 | 1.03 | 1.30 | 0.98 | 0.65 |

    Which of the following options shows the numbers in order from smallest to largest?
    - **A** 0.35  0.98  0.65  1.30  1.03
    - **B** 0.35  0.65  0.98  1.03  1.30
    - **C** 1.30  1.03  0.98  0.65  0.35
    - **D** 0.35  0.65  0.98  1.30  1.03
    - **E** 1.03  1.30  0.98  0.65  0.35

/ 5

6. Which of these triangles is an equilateral triangle?

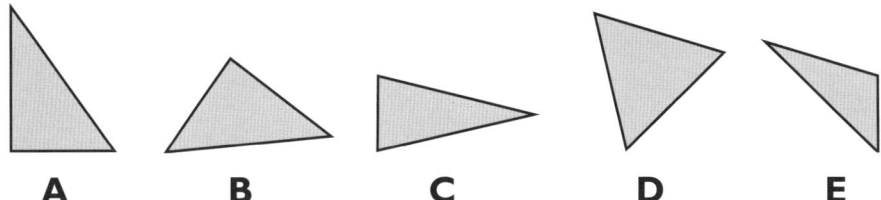

7. Max is facing north. He turns to face south.

   How many right angles has he turned through?

   Answer: _____

8. Which of these shapes has a line of symmetry?

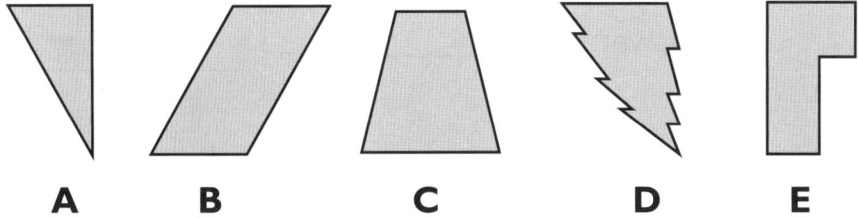

9. Sarah visits her grandma every Sunday.
   She visits on 12th February.

   What is the date of the next Sunday she will visit her grandma?

   **A** 5th February  **C** 17th February  **E** 19th February
   **B** 12th March    **D** 20th February

10. ☐ < 4652

    Which of the following numbers could go in the box above?

    **A** 4731  **B** 4599  **C** 5120  **D** 4655  **E** 6021

11. John records the maximum temperature in Aberdeen each day for a week. He draws this bar chart to show his results.

    What is the difference between the temperature on Wednesday and on Saturday?

    Answer: _____ °C

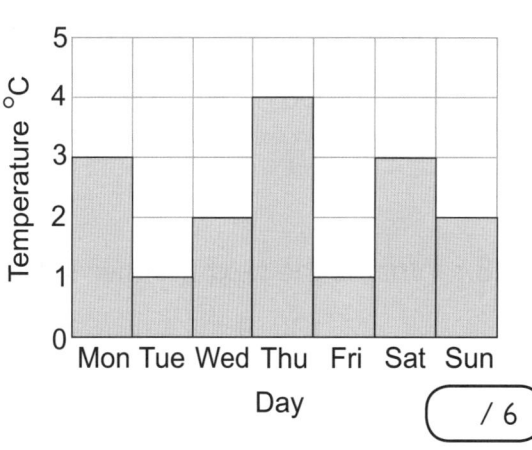

Carry on to the next question → →

12. $\boxed{60 - 37 = 23}$

    What is 560 – 237?  Answer: _____

13. What is 4500 ÷ 100?

    **A** 400.5  **B** 0.45  **C** 4.5  **D** 45  **E** 450

14. Class 4C counted the vehicles that passed by the window during their maths lesson. They put the results on this pictogram.

    How many buses and motorbikes did they see in total?

    Answer: _____

    | Lorry | |
    |---|---|
    | Car | |
    | Motorbike | |
    | Bus | |

    ● = 4 vehicles

15. Apples come in packs of 6.
    Ted's class need to buy enough packs so that each child can have one apple.
    There are 32 children in the class.

    How many packs of apples will they need?

    **A** 5  **B** 6  **C** 8  **D** 4  **E** 7

16. £87 is shared equally between three people.

    How much money do they each receive?

    Answer: £ _____

17. What is 5240 rounded to the nearest hundred?

    **A** 10 000  **B** 5300  **C** 5270  **D** 5200  **E** 5000

18. What is the next number in this sequence?

    13  9  5  1  –3  ?

    **A** –1  **B** –5  **C** –6  **D** –7  **E** 1

    /7

Assessment Test 2

19. ¾ of the grid on the right is shaded.
Which of the fractions below is equal to ¾?

A  14/16   B  10/16   C  12/16   D  7/16   E  4/16

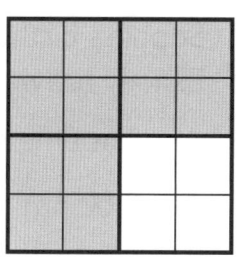

20. Which corner of the pentagon is at point (1, 4)?

Answer: _____

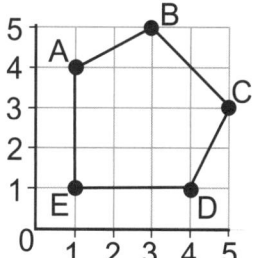

21. How many grams are there in 2½ kilograms?

A  250 g   B  25 g   C  2500 g   D  2050 g   E  2.5 g

22. This is a diagram of Azra's trampoline.
It is a regular hexagon.

What is the perimeter of the trampoline?

Answer: _____ m

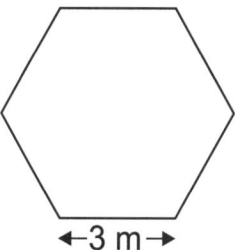

23. Tom is making a pattern of squares using counters.

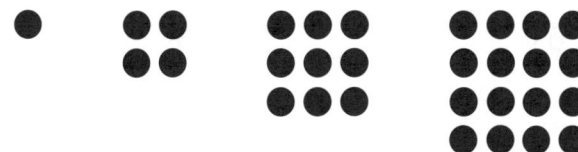

How many counters will he need to make the next square in the pattern?

A  20   B  25   C  30   D  35   E  36

24. Vikram's dog weighs 16 kg.
He uses this table to work out how many biscuits to feed his dog each day.

How many biscuits should Vikram give his dog in a week?

A  14   C  15   E  28
B  7    D  29

| Dog weight | Number of biscuits a day |
|---|---|
| Up to 7 kg | 1 |
| Up to 15 kg | 2 |
| Up to 30 kg | 4 |

25. Sophie's birthday party starts at 4 pm and finishes at 6:30 pm.
    Exactly halfway through the party the children have the birthday cake.

    At what time do they have the cake?

    A  5:00 pm     C  5:15 pm     E  6:00 pm
    B  5:30 pm     D  5:45 pm

26. Noel's family go to the cinema.

    How much does it cost for 3 children and 2 adults?

    Answer: £ _____

    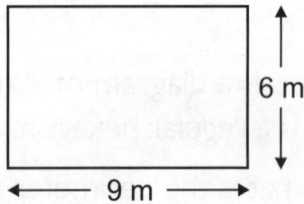

    Cinema tickets
    Child  £3.50
    Adult  £7.50

27. This is a diagram of Adam's vegetable garden.

    What is its area?

    A  54 m²     C  15 m²     E  56 m²
    B  81 m²     D  30 m²

28. A packet of raisins weighs 65 g.

    What do 6 packets of raisins weigh to the nearest 100 g?

    A  300 g    B  400 g    C  200 g    D  500 g    E  390 g

29. A horse has 250 ml of medicine every day.
    There are 2 litres of medicine in the bottle.

    How many days will the bottle of medicine last for?

    Answer: _____ days

    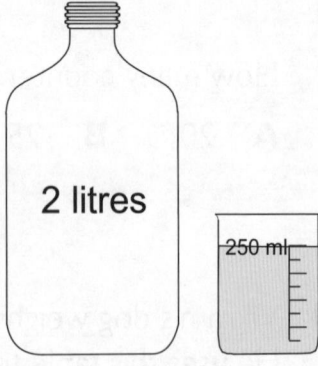

30. A stall sells hot dogs for £1.25 each.
    Dee buys 3 hot dogs and pays with a £10 note.

    How much change does she get?

    A  £5.25    B  £7.52    C  £6.25    D  £7.25    E  £6.50

    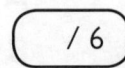

    **End of Test**

Assessment Test 2

# Assessment Test 3

Allow 35 minutes to do this test. Work as quickly and as carefully as you can.

You can print **multiple-choice answer sheets** for these questions from our website — go to cgpbooks.co.uk/11plus/answer-sheets or scan the QR code on the right. If you'd prefer to answer them in standard write-in format, either write your answers in the spaces provided or circle the **correct answer** from the options **A** to **E**.

1. What type of shape is this?

   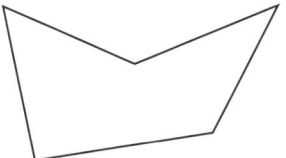

   **A** hexagon     **C** octagon     **E** triangle
   **B** pentagon     **D** square

2. Write the number three thousand and seventeen in figures.     Answer: _____

3. Omar's class are split into teams of 5 children. There are 30 children in the class. How many teams are there?

   **A** 8    **B** 6    **C** 4    **D** 7    **E** 5

4. Find the difference between 59 and 73.     Answer: _____

5. Class 4 made this pictogram to show the animals they saw on their country walk.

   How many sheep did they see?

   Answer: _____

   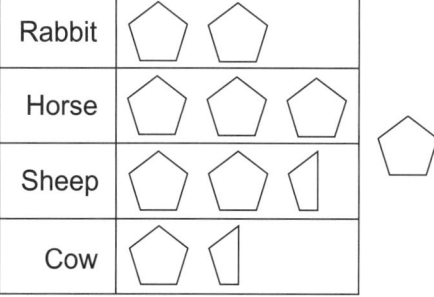

6. How many lines of symmetry does this equilateral triangle have?

   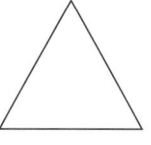

   **A** 3    **B** 4    **C** 2    **D** 6    **E** 1

/ 6

**Carry on to the next question → →**

7. Edward draws this bar chart to show the favourite sports of children in his year group.

   Which sport did fewest children choose?

   Answer: _____

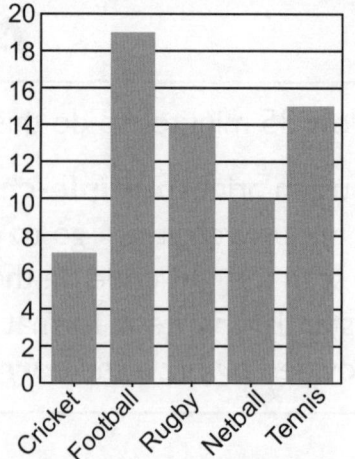

8. Which of the following pairs of numbers are both multiples of 9?

   **A** 90 and 72
   **B** 27 and 42
   **C** 14 and 36
   **D** 62 and 15
   **E** 56 and 18

9. What fraction of the hexagon is shaded?

   **A** 1/6  **B** 1/5  **C** 5/6  **D** 1/7  **E** 1/4

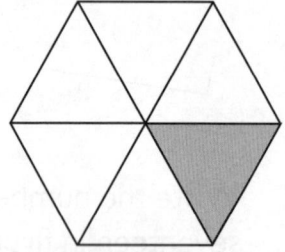

10. Angle *y* is smaller than a right angle.

    Which of the following could be the size of angle *y*?

    **A** 120°  **C** 170°  **E** 180°
    **B** 40°   **D** 90°

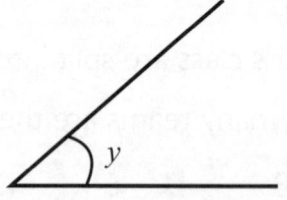

11. What number is the arrow pointing to on this number line?

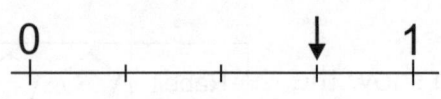

    **A** 0.25  **B** 0.5  **C** 7.5  **D** 0.75  **E** 0.33

12. The thermometer shows the temperature on a hilltop. The temperature is 3 °C warmer at the bottom of the hill.

    What is the temperature at the bottom of the hill?

    Answer: _____ °C

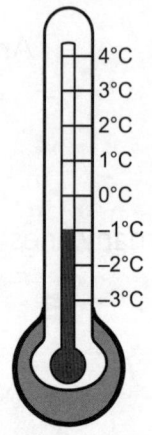

/ 6

Assessment Test 3

13. How many pence are there in £2.35?

    Answer: _____ p

14. The diagram shows part of a map of a zoo.

    Aki is visiting the giraffes.
    In which direction must he walk to reach the elephants?

    A  south-west     C  east     E  south-east
    B  west           D  south

15. Which one of the following times is the same as twenty minutes to three?

    A  2:40     B  2:50     C  3:45     D  3:40     E  3:20

16. This is a diagram of a school stage.

    What is its perimeter?

    Answer: _____ m

    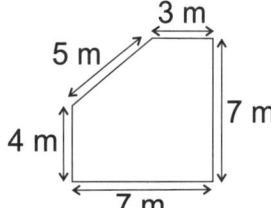

17. The diagram shows a square-based pyramid.

    How many faces does it have?

    Answer: _____

    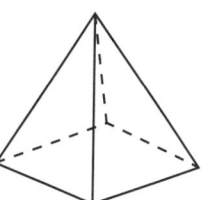

18. Look at this bus timetable.
    Denise catches the bus in Shipford. She gets off at Uptown.
    How long is her bus journey?

    Answer: _____ minutes

    | Bus stop | Time |
    | --- | --- |
    | Markham | 8:20 am |
    | Shipford | 8:28 am |
    | Uptown | 8:46 am |

    / 6

    Carry on to the next question → →

    Assessment Test 3

19. Katy thinks of a number. She multiplies it by 4 and gets 88.

    What number was Katy thinking of?

    **A** 44  **B** 92  **C** 84  **D** 22  **E** 352

20. What is £1.50 more than £36.90?  Answer: £ _____

21. Saroo started with the number 3 and used the rule "add 4" to make a sequence. What is the 5th number in her sequence?

    **A** 7  **C** 17  **E** 20
    **B** 15  **D** 19

22. What is 37 × 4?  Answer: _____

23. Fiona is making ice cubes for a party.
    She uses 10 ml of water to make one ice cube.

    How many ice cubes can she make from one litre of water?

    **A** 1000  **B** 10 000  **C** 10  **D** 1  **E** 100

24. Mr Tran is making a path through his vegetable patch using hexagonal stones.

    Before lunch he lays a third of the stones.
    The diagram shows the path so far.

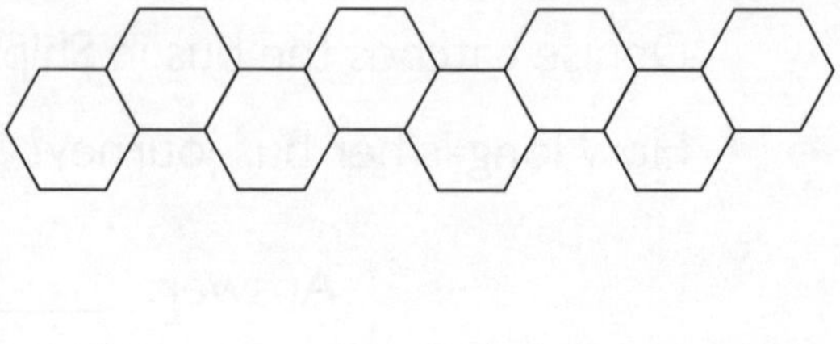

    How many stones will be in the finished path?

    Answer: _____

Assessment Test 3

25. Freya buys a glass of juice and a cookie.

    How much change does she get from £5.00?

    A  £3.19      C  £2.91      E  £2.19
    B  £3.91      D  £2.10

26. Which of these numbers does not equal 480 when it is rounded to the nearest 10?

    A  485     B  475     C  480.5     D  478     E  484.5

27. Look at the rectangles on the right.

    Which two rectangles have the same area?

    Answer: _____ and _____

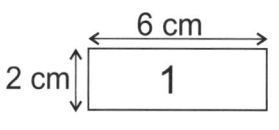
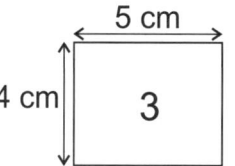
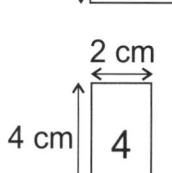

28. The ingredients for a salad for 4 people are shown on the right.
    Mika wants to make it for 12 people.

    How much olive oil should she use?

    A  45 ml      C  90 ml      E  135 ml
    B  15 ml      D  450 ml

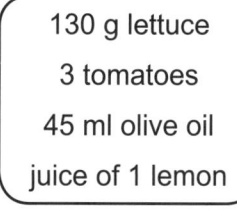

29. What are the coordinates of the point marked A?

    Answer: ( _____ , _____ )

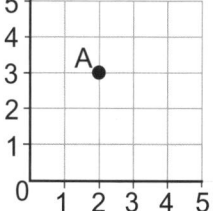

30. Henry is measuring the width of the school tennis court using his stride.
    His stride measures 80 centimetres. The court is 9 strides wide.

    What is the width of the court to the nearest metre?

    A  7 m     B  9 m     C  72 m     D  6 m     E  8 m

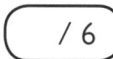

**End of Test**

Assessment Test 3

# Assessment Test 4

Allow 35 minutes to do this test. Work as quickly and as carefully as you can.

You can print **multiple-choice answer sheets** for these questions from our website — go to cgpbooks.co.uk/11plus/answer-sheets or scan the QR code on the right. If you'd prefer to answer them in standard write-in format, either write your answers in the spaces provided or circle the **correct answer** from the options **A** to **E**.

1. Which of these shapes is a hexagon?

   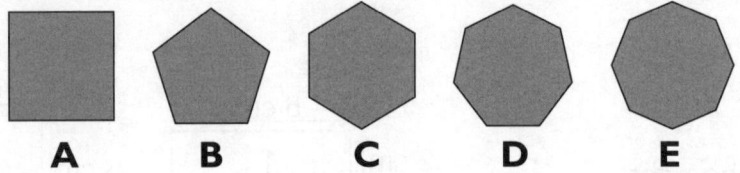

   A    B    C    D    E

2. Which of the following is the most likely weight of an apple?

   **A** 0.3 g    **B** 3 g    **C** 0.3 kg    **D** 3 kg    **E** 30 kg

3. Which of these numbers is the smallest?

   4.70    40.7    0.47    7.4    70.4        Answer: _____

4. Look at this list of numbers.

   18    30    15    12    36

   Which of the following numbers is a factor of all the numbers in the list?

   **A** 2    **B** 3    **C** 4    **D** 5    **E** 6

5. What is the sum of all the even numbers between 1 and 9?

   **A** 20    **B** 36    **C** 45    **D** 16    **E** 50

6. Which of these shapes has only one line of symmetry?

   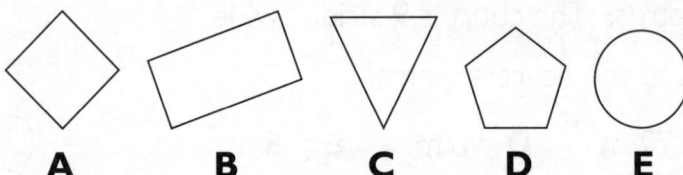

   A    B    C    D    E

/ 6

7. This pictogram shows the numbers of sweets sold by a shop in one day.

| Sweet | Number sold |
|---|---|
| Chocolate mice | 🍬 🍬 🍬 🍬 |
| Sherbert discs | 🍬 🍬 |
| Lollipops | 🍬 🍬 🍬 🍬 🍬 |
| Foam bananas | 🍬 🍬 🍬 🍬 |
| Strawberry laces | 🍬 🍬 🍬 |

🍬 = 6 sweets

How many strawberry laces were sold?

Answer: _____

8. What is $\frac{1}{4}$ of 32?

Answer: _____

9. There are 24 children in a class.
Every child in the class needs one of each type of book shown in the bar chart.

Which books are there not enough of?

A  Maths and Art
B  Music only
C  History and Music
D  History and English
E  Music, History and English

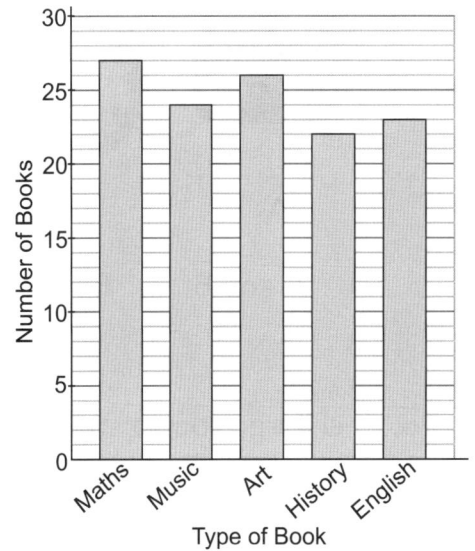

10. How many centimetres are there in 17.04 metres?

A  170 400 cm      D  170.4 cm
B  170 40 cm       E  170.04 cm
C  1704 cm

11. The temperature in Norway is −5 °C.
The temperature in Dubai is 26 °C.

What is the difference between these two temperatures?

Answer: _____ °C

12. A teacher wants to split 56 children into teams of 6.

How many complete teams can he make?

Answer: _____

Carry on to the next question → →

Assessment Test 4

13. Which of these numbers should go in the area labelled X on this Venn diagram?

    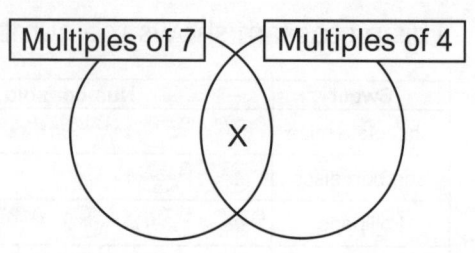

    A  14     D  35
    B  21     E  43
    C  28

14. What number is the arrow pointing to on this number line?

    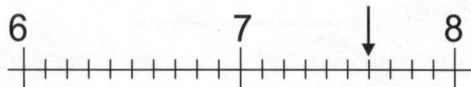

    Answer: _____

15. Which two clocks show the same time?

    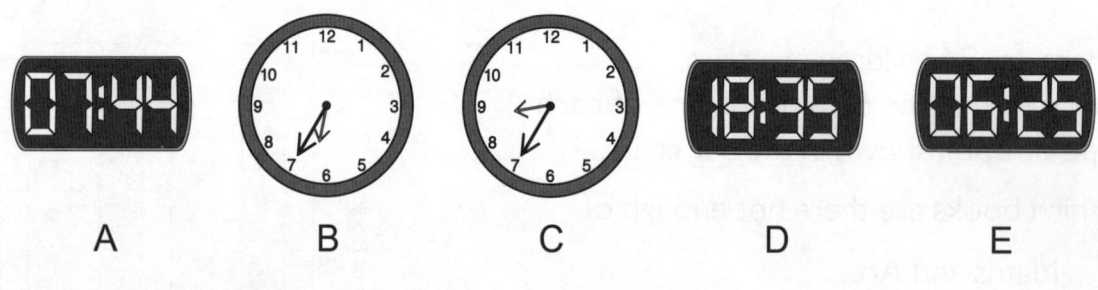

    A  A and B    B  A and D    C  A and C    D  B and D    E  B and E

16. 5 children took a spelling test.
    The table shows their marks rounded to the nearest 10.

    Which child could have scored 74 in the test?

    A  Paul       D  Hemish
    B  Kirsty     E  Fiona
    C  Leon

    | Name | Rounded Mark |
    | --- | --- |
    | Paul | 80 |
    | Kirsty | 50 |
    | Leon | 100 |
    | Hemish | 70 |
    | Fiona | 60 |

17. Which two of these diagrams have the same fraction shaded?

    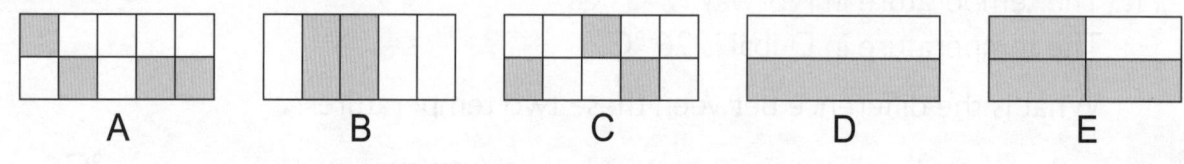

    A  D and E    B  A and E    C  A and B    D  C and D    E  B and E

18. Which of these numbers is closest to 5000?

    A  4892    B  5029    C  4972    D  5100    E  4962

Assessment Test 4

19. Estimate the size of angle *a* in this shape.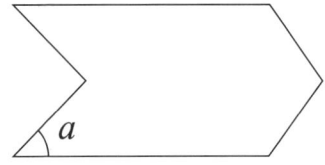

    A  90°      D  45°
    B  100°     E  180°
    C  120°

20. What is the total cost of 7 pens sold at 99p each?

    Answer: £ _____

21. Ranji buys a loaf of bread and three cans of cola.
    He pays a total of £3.00.  The shop charges 90p for a loaf of bread.

    How much does one can of cola cost?

    Answer: _____ p

22. What is the missing digit in this calculation?

    1 ☐ × 8 = 120

    A  4      B  5      C  6      D  7      E  8

23. This is a net for a 3D shape.  What shape will
    it make if it is folded along the dashed lines?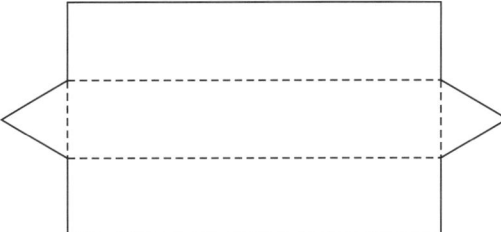

    A  A cuboid
    B  A triangular prism
    C  A square-based pyramid
    D  A polygon
    E  A quadrilateral

24. A rectangle is split in half into two triangles.

    What type of triangle must each of these triangles be?

    A  Scalene triangles         D  Isosceles triangles
    B  Right-angled triangles    E  Quadrilateral triangles
    C  Equilateral triangles

25. Lindsey writes a list of numbers.
    She starts with the number 13 and counts backwards in steps of 4.

    Which of these numbers will be on her list?

    A  8      B  4      C  0      D  –3      E  –8

Carry on to the next question → →

Assessment Test 4

26. This table shows the amount of money collected by each stall at a fair.

| Stall | Money Collected | |
|---|---|---|
| | Morning | Afternoon |
| Tombola | £18.00 | £11.00 |
| Coconut Shy | £15.00 | £17.00 |
| Penalty Shoot-out | £16.00 | £22.00 |
| Pony Ride | £21.00 | £19.00 |
| Bash the Rat | £13.00 | £20.00 |

Which stall collected the most money over the whole day?

**A** Tombola  **D** Pony Ride
**B** Coconut Shy  **E** Bash the Rat
**C** Penalty Shoot-out

27. Esther buys a box of 100 ice pops for £36. She works out how much each ice pop cost her to buy and sells each ice pop for 14p more than this amount.

How much money does Esther sell each ice pop for?

Answer: _____ p

28. Sasha thinks of a number. She multiplies the number by 8, then adds 3. The number she ends up with is 51.

What number did Sasha start with?

Answer: _____

29. Sandeep measures the length of the playground with a stick. The playground is 30 stick lengths long. The stick is 55 cm long.

How long is the playground?

**A** 16.5 m  **B** 165 m  **C** 65 m  **D** 160 cm  **E** 1650 m

30. Points A, B and C lie on the corners of a rectangle. Point D lies on the fourth corner of the rectangle.

What are the coordinates of point D?

**A** (7, 5)  **D** (2, 8)
**B** (8, 4)  **E** (4, 8)
**C** (5, 7)

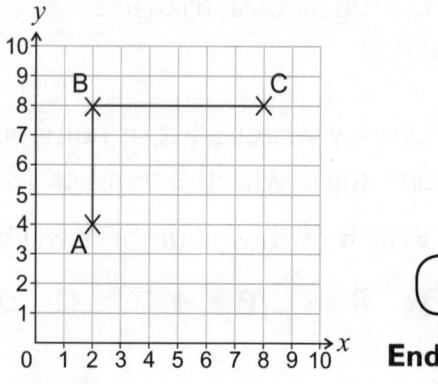

**End of Test**

Assessment Test 4

# Assessment Test 5

Allow 35 minutes to do this test. Work as quickly and as carefully as you can.

You can print **multiple-choice answer sheets** for these questions from our website — go to cgpbooks.co.uk/11plus/answer-sheets or scan the QR code on the right. If you'd prefer to answer them in standard write-in format, either write your answers in the spaces provided or circle the **correct answer** from the options **A** to **E**.

1. Which number is in the wrong section of this Venn diagram?

   Answer: _____

   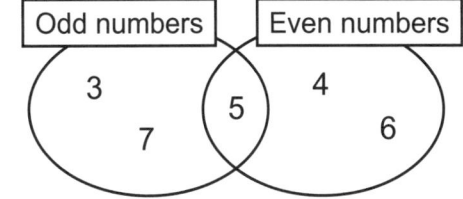

2. Mr Button is buying some tiles for his bathroom. He wants tiles which have 5 equal sides.

   What shape should his tiles be?

   A circle
   B regular hexagon
   C triangle
   D regular pentagon
   E square

3. One minibus has space for 9 passengers.

   How many minibuses are needed for 72 passengers?

   A 8   B 6   C 12   D 7   E 15

4. Chris is making flapjacks. The scales show the weight of the sugar that he uses.

   How much sugar does Chris use?

   Answer: _____ g

   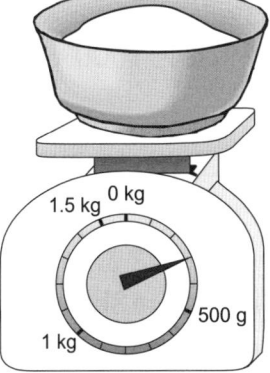

5. Which of the following is the most likely height of a house?

   A 0.85 km
   B 850 mm
   C 8.5 m
   D 85 cm
   E 80.5 m

/ 5

Carry on to the next question → →

6. Which pair of numbers can go in the shaded box of the table?

   A  8 and 12    D  6 and 8
   B  7 and 9     E  9 and 10
   C  3 and 6

|      | odd numbers | even numbers |
|------|-------------|--------------|
| >10  | 11  15      | 12  20       |
| <10  | 3  5        |              |

7. What fraction of this shape is shaded?

   A  3/12    C  7/12    E  8/12
   B  5/12    D  4/12

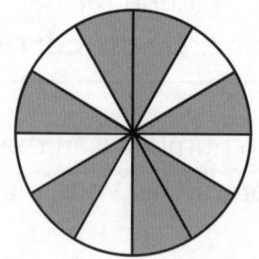

8. Which of these numbers is not a multiple of 3 and 5?

   A  15    B  30    C  35    D  60    E  45

9. Round 17.48 m to the nearest 0.1 m.

   Answer: _____ m

10. One 20p coin weighs 5 g.

    How much will 20p coins worth £1 weigh?

    A  25 g    B  125 g    C  1.25 kg    D  250 g    E  2.5 kg

11. What is 1000 − 567?

    A  437    B  441    C  563    D  433    E  537

12. The table shows the temperature in Antarctica on five days.

    What was the difference in temperature between Wednesday and Thursday?

    A  6 °C     D  4 °C
    B  7 °C     E  5 °C
    C  12 °C

| Day       | Temperature (°C) |
|-----------|------------------|
| Monday    | −6               |
| Tuesday   | −4               |
| Wednesday | −7               |
| Thursday  | −12              |
| Friday    | −8               |

/7

Assessment Test 5

13. ☐ ÷ 8 = 70

    What is the missing number in this calculation?

    Answer: _____

14. The pictogram shows the scores of five teams in a quiz.

    What is the difference between the scores of Team 2 and Team 5?

    Answer: _____ points

    ★ = 6 points

    | Team 1 | ★ ★ ★ |
    | Team 2 | ★ ★ |
    | Team 3 | ★ ★ ★ ★ ⤳ |
    | Team 4 | ★ ◊ |
    | Team 5 | ★ ★ ★ ⤳ |

15. A train leaves Birmingham at 8:57 and arrives in Manchester at 10:45.

    How long did the journey take?

    A  2 hours and 48 minutes
    B  1 hour and 45 minutes
    C  2 hours and 12 minutes
    D  1 hour and 48 minutes
    E  1 hour and 42 minutes

16. Aaron is laying concrete blocks to make a path. Each block weighs 3 kg.

    How much would three blocks weigh in grams?

    A  90 g     B  9000 g     C  9.9 g     D  900 g     E  3000 g

17. Point P on the grid is moved three squares down and two squares right.

    Which option below gives the correct coordinates of the new position of point P?

    A        B        C        D        E
    (6, 3)   (2, 3)   (7, 4)   (3, 6)   (4, 7)

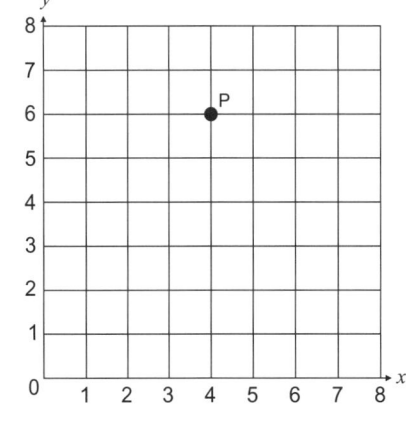

18. Here is a part of a sequence:

    ...12, 24, 48, 96...

    The rule for the sequence is 'double the previous number'.

    Which number came before 12 in the sequence?

    Answer: _____

    / 6

    Carry on to the next question → →

19. Akmal folds up a net to make a cube.

    Which of the following nets could he have used?

    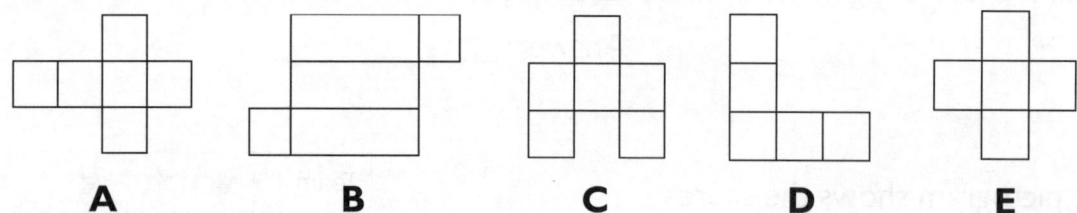

    A  B  C  D  E

20. Shape X is reflected in a vertical mirror line.

    Which of the following shapes is the reflection of shape X?

    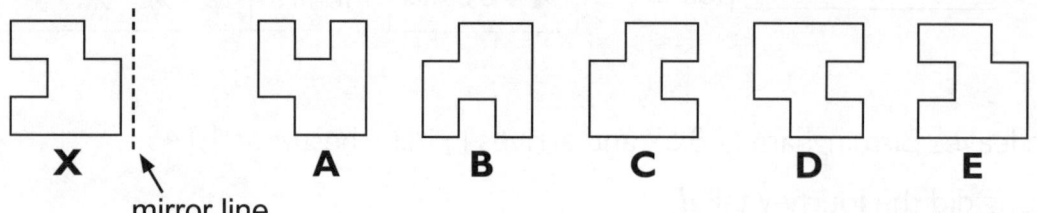

    X    A    B    C    D    E
    
    mirror line

21. Kirsten's bookshelf is 1 m long.
    She has some books which are all 7 cm thick.

    How many books can she fit on her bookshelf?

    **A** 7    **B** 15    **C** 13    **D** 14    **E** 16

22. The bar chart shows the height of six buildings.

    What is the difference in height between building 3 and building 5?

    Answer: _____ m

    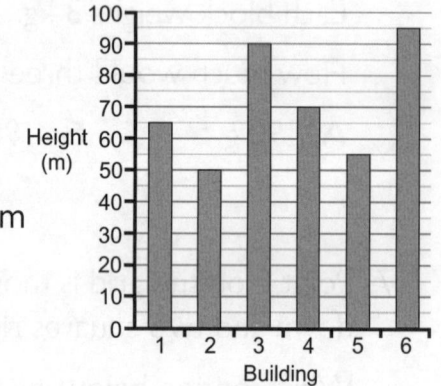

23. Kaya buys 4 oranges at 49p each.
    She pays with a £10 note.

    What change will she be given?

    **A** £1.96    **C** £7.62    **E** £4.90
    **B** £8.04    **D** £9.02

24. Liz makes this shape using six white cubes.
    She paints the outside of the shape blue and
    then breaks the shape apart into cubes again.

    How many cube faces are white?

    **A** 10    **B** 12    **C** 8    **D** 5    **E** 7

    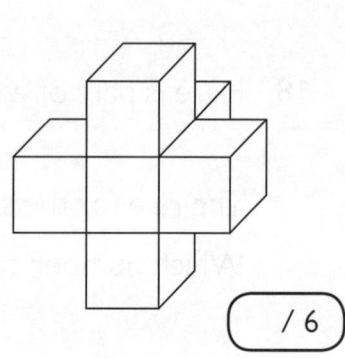

Assessment Test 5

25. A jug contains 3 litres of water. Maxine pours six 200 ml glasses of water from the jug.

    How much water is left in the jug?

    A  1200 ml    C  600 ml    E  1500 ml
    B  1800 ml    D  2400 ml

26. Which of these statements is true?
    A  A cube has four faces.
    B  A triangle-based pyramid has one rectangular face.
    C  A square-based pyramid has four triangular faces.
    D  A cylinder has no curved faces.
    E  A triangular prism has three triangular faces.

27. Each chapter in a book is eight pages long.
    Susi reads the first 8 chapters and 5 pages of chapter 9.

    How many pages has Susi read?        Answer: _____ pages

28. Alia's cat eats 85 g of tinned meat a day.

    How much tinned meat does her cat eat in a week?

    A  705 g    B  560 g    C  635 g    D  595 g    E  460 g

29. The battery of Darren's mobile phone lasts for 50 hours before he has to charge it again. The battery is fully charged at 9 am on Sunday morning.

    When will Darren have to charge the battery again?

    A  1 pm Tuesday         D  11 am Tuesday
    B  11 pm Monday         E  5 am Wednesday
    C  11 am Wednesday

30. Harvey draws points A and B on this coordinate grid. He draws point C and then draws a line between points B and C to make a right angle.

    Which of the following could be the coordinates of point C?

    A  (2, 4)    C  (2, 1)    E  (5, 4)
    B  (3, 2)    D  (3, 3)

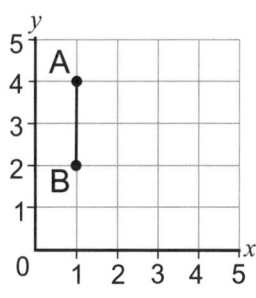

**End of Test**

Assessment Test 5

# Assessment Test 6

Allow 35 minutes to do this test. Work as quickly and as carefully as you can.

You can print **multiple-choice answer sheets** for these questions from our website — go to cgpbooks.co.uk/11plus/answer-sheets or scan the QR code on the right. If you'd prefer to answer them in standard write-in format, either write your answers in the spaces provided or circle the **correct answer** from the options **A** to **E**.

Answer Sheets

1. Which of these numbers is the largest?

   113   134   3.4   13   34

   Answer: _____

2. The bar chart shows the amount of rain on an island during the first six months of a year.

   Which month had the highest amount of rain?

   Answer: _____

   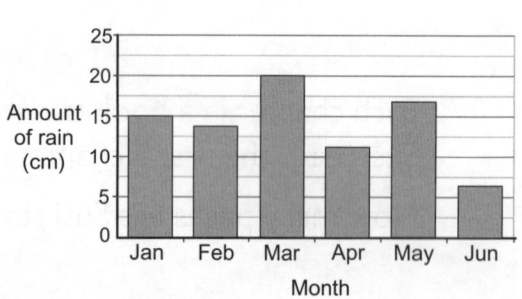

3. What number is 110 less than 1000?

   **A** 880   **B** 910   **C** 990   **D** 890   **E** 900

4. Mick adds up the 7 digits on this barcode.

   What answer does he get?

   Answer: _____

   0 5 1 5 6 4 7

5. There are 606 chickens at Raven Farm.
   There are 149 fewer chickens at Shrove Farm.

   How many chickens are there at Shrove Farm?

   **A** 567   **B** 457   **C** 543   **D** 467   **E** 563

6. Which of these weights is closest to 3 kg?

   **A** 3.2 kg   **B** 2.8 kg   **C** 2.9 kg   **D** 2.5 kg   **E** 3.3 kg

/ 6

7. The pictogram shows the number of hours of sunshine on five days.

   How many more hours of sunshine were there on Thursday than on Monday?

   Answer: _____ hours

   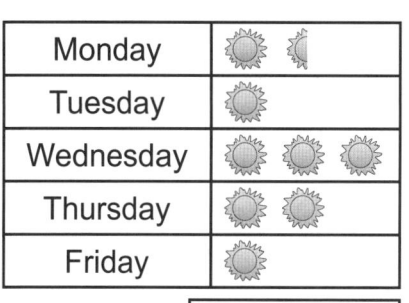

8. Which pair of numbers have a difference of 13?

   **A** 61 and 55    **C** 44 and 56    **E** 34 and 48
   **B** 77 and 91    **D** 58 and 71

9. Olivia draws this triangle on a coordinate grid.

   Which of these squares is not inside the triangle?

   **A** C3    **C** E5    **E** F7
   **B** D5    **D** D2

   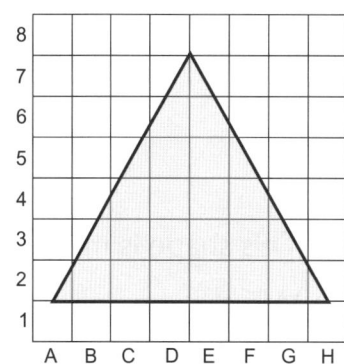

10. Taj starts at 17 and counts back in steps of 5.

    Which of these numbers will be in his sequence?

    **A** 1    **B** 2    **C** 3    **D** 4    **E** 5

11. Which number is in the wrong section of this Venn diagram?

    Answer: _____

    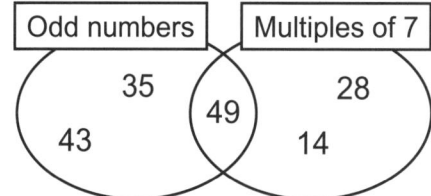

12. A TV programme starts at 17:45 and lasts for 57 minutes.

    What time does the programme finish?

    **A** 18:48    **B** 6:43    **C** 18:42    **D** 16:42    **E** 19:48

13. Anne-Marie can make 4 necklaces out of 320 beads. Each necklace has the same amount of beads.

    How many beads are there in each necklace?

    **A** 90    **C** 80    **E** 140
    **B** 160   **D** 100

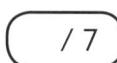

Carry on to the next question → →

14. Priya draws this shape on some squared paper. Each square on the paper has an area of 1 cm².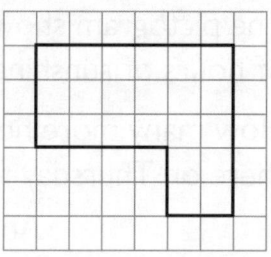

    What is the area of Priya's shape?

    A  22 cm²   C  15 cm²   E  18 cm²
    B  10 cm²   D  24 cm²

15. Which of these is equal to 120?

    A  121 to the nearest 100
    B  117 to the nearest 10
    C  12 to the nearest 100
    D  119.4 to the nearest whole number
    E  125 to the nearest 10

16. This shape is made from five identical rectangles.

    What is the perimeter of the shape?

    Answer: _____ cm

17. A postcard costs 40p. Nikki buys three postcards.

    How much change does she receive from £5?

    A  £1.20   C  £4.60   E  £4.20
    B  £3.80   D  £4.00

18. What is 90 × 9?

    A  999   C  900   E  810
    B  891   D  890

19. Which pair of values are equal?

    A  0.1 and ¼      C  ¾ and 0.25     E  ½ and 0.5
    B  ³⁄₁₀ and 0.4   D  ⁷⁄₁₀ and 0.5

/ 6

Assessment Test 6

20. A car uses 2 litres of fuel to travel 12 miles.

    How many litres of fuel will the car need to travel 72 miles?

    Answer: _____ litres

21. Brian made this bar chart to record how much his plant grew each week.

    How much did the plant grow in total during weeks 4, 5 and 6?

    Answer: _____ cm

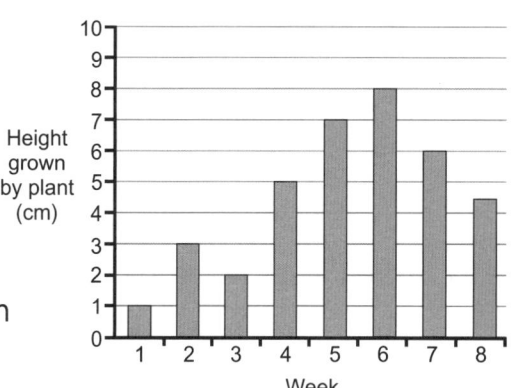

22. Ada bought a bag containing 15 marbles. She gave 1/5 of the marbles to Jenni.

    How many marbles did Ada have left?

    **A** 12    **B** 3    **C** 10    **D** 5    **E** 9

23. Chelsea reflected this rectangle in the mirror line.

    Which point shows the reflection of point Z?

    **A**    **B**    **C**    **D**    **E**

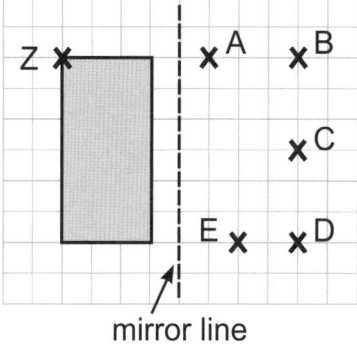

mirror line

24. Look at the two jugs of orange juice shown on the right.

    How much orange juice is there in total?

    **A** 2500 ml    **C** 3050 ml    **E** 2650 ml
    **B** 2150 ml    **D** 3500 ml

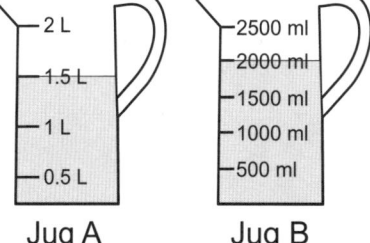

25. Which of these nets will fold up to make a square-based pyramid?

 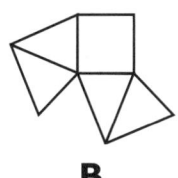 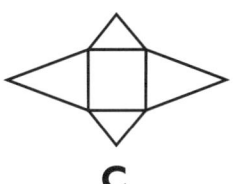 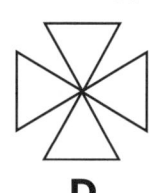 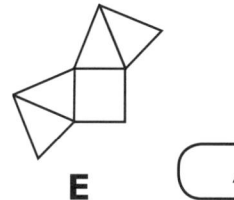

**A**    **B**    **C**    **D**    **E**

26. A shop keeps ice cream in a freezer at −16 °C.
The freezer breaks down at 4 am and the temperature in the freezer rises by 1 °C every hour.

At what time will the temperature in the freezer reach −9 °C?

A  10 am    C  1 pm    E  9 am
B  7 am     D  11 am

27. Wen glues five cubes together to make this shape.

How many faces do not have glue on them?

A  22    C  16    E  24
B  20    D  17

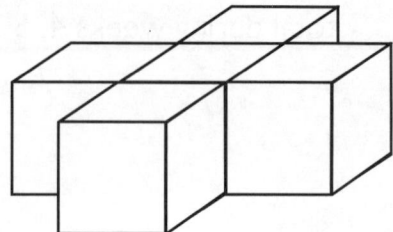

28. Tickets to a theme park cost £9.50.
8 friends go to the theme park.

How much do they spend on their tickets in total?

Answer: £ _____

29. Mara bought a block of cheese and two packs of butter. The three items weighed 920 g in total. The block of cheese weighed 470 g.

What is the weight of one pack of butter?

Answer: _____ g

30. Mr Green started filling in this table to record the number of children from Years 4 and 5 who were going on a school trip.

How many Year 4 girls went on the trip?

Answer: _____

|  | Year 4 | Year 5 | Total |
|---|---|---|---|
| Boys | 22 | 9 | 31 |
| Girls | ? |  | 28 |
| Total |  | 26 | 59 |

/ 5

**End of Test**

Assessment Test 6

# Answers

## Section One — Number Knowledge

### Pages 2-3

Compare the place value of the digits in the options. Start with the value of the digits on the left. If these have the same place value and are the same number, compare the values of the next lot of digits to the right until you find the smallest number.

1) 50
2) 890
3) 114
4) 1230
5) 2.4

Find the difference between two given numbers on the number line. Divide the difference by the number of sections between those numbers to find how much the number line increases by at each point. Then you just need to count along the points from a number you're given to the number the arrow is pointing at.

6) 14
The number line is marked in 1s.

7) 6
The number line is marked in 2s.

8) 80
The number line is marked in 5s.

9) 19
The number line is marked in 1s.

10) 65
The number line is marked in 5s.

Count how many places the 7 is from the left or right of the decimal point to work out its place value.

11) Hundreds
The 7 is three places to the left of the decimal point, so it's in the hundreds column.

12) Units
The 7 is one place to the left of the decimal point, so it's in the units column.

13) Units
The 7 is one place to the left of the decimal point, so it's in the units column.

14) Tenths
The 7 is one place to the right of the decimal point, so it's in the tenths column.

15) Hundredths
The 7 is two places to the right of the decimal point, so it's in the hundredths column.

16) 7532
To make the largest number possible you need to arrange the digits in order from largest to smallest — 7532.

17) John
The shortest time is the smallest number. Compare the place value of the digits in the options. Start with the value of the digits on the left. If these are the same, then compare the value of the next lot of digits to the right until you find the smallest number. The smallest number is 108 seconds (John).

18) 1.02 m
The smallest person's height is the smallest number. Start with the value of the digits on the left. If these are the same, then compare the value of the next lot of digits to the right until you find the smallest number. This is 1.02 m.

19) E
The difference between 2.4 and 3.8 is 3.8 − 2.4 = 1.4. Half of 1.4 is 0.7, so the middle value is 0.7 away from 2.4 and 3.8. The middle value is 3.1 — option E

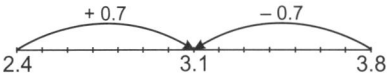

20) 3
Mr Pearson can only travel with airlines that have a maximum luggage weight above 20.08 kg. 20.2 kg (Air Kings), 20.14 kg (Fly by Night) and 20.4 kg (Pronto Planes) have a maximum luggage weight above 20.08 kg.

21) D
Both 15 and 23 are 4 away from 19. 15 + 4 = 19 and 23 − 4 = 19.

22) E
Look for the biggest number under 1000 and the smallest number above 1000. Then look at the difference between 1000 and these two numbers. The difference between 997.5 and 1000 is 1000 − 997.5 = 2.5. The difference between 1002.9 and 1000 is 1002.9 − 1000 = 2.9. So 997.5 is closest to 1000.

23) B
Both 6.4 and 5.6 are 0.4 away from 6. 6.4 − 0.4 = 6 and 5.6 + 0.4 = 6.

### Pages 4-5

Look at the two possible answers that you would round up or down to. Find the value that is halfway between them. If the number you're rounding is less than the halfway value, round down. If it is equal to or more than the halfway value, round up.

1) 70
75 is halfway between 70 and 80. 71 is less than 75, so 71 rounds down to 70.

2) 350
345 is halfway between 340 and 350. 349 is more than 345, so 349 rounds up to 350.

3) 410
405 is halfway between 400 and 410. 407 is more than 405, so 407 rounds up to 410.

4) 1540
1535 is halfway between 1530 and 1540. 1536 is more than 1535, so 1536 rounds up to 1540.

5) 3090
3095 is halfway between 3090 and 3100. 3092 is less than 3095, so 3092 rounds down to 3090.

6) 1300
1250 is halfway between 1200 and 1300. 1295.61 is more than 1250, so 1295.61 rounds up to 1300.

7) 1295.6
1295.65 is halfway between 1295.6 and 1295.7. 1295.61 is less than 1295.65, so 1295.61 rounds down to 1295.6.

**8) 1300**
1295 is halfway between 1290 and 1300. 1295.61 is more than 1295, so 1295.61 rounds up to 1300.

**9) 1296**
1295.5 is halfway between 1295 and 1296. 1295.61 is more than 1295.5, so 1295.61 rounds up to 1296.

The numbers that have been rounded to the nearest 10 end in one zero. If it ends in two zeros then it has been rounded to the nearest 100, and if it ends in three zeros then it has been rounded to the nearest 1000.

**10) 10**
30 ends in one zero, so 25 has been rounded to the nearest 10.

**11) 100**
400 ends in two zeros, so 381 has been rounded to the nearest 100.

**12) 10**
620 ends in one zero, so 615 has been rounded to the nearest 10.

**13) 1000**
1000 ends in three zeros, so 1247 has been rounded to the nearest 1000.

**14) 100**
500 ends in two zeros, so 517.4 has been rounded to the nearest 100.

**15) £6.00**
£6.50 is halfway between £6.00 and £7.00.
£6.27 is less than £6.50, so £6.27 rounds down to £6.00.

**16) 210**
215 is halfway between 210 and 220.
212 is less than 215, so 212 rounds down to 210.

**17) 3300**
3250 is halfway between 3200 and 3300.
3264 is more than 3250, so 3264 rounds up to 3300.

**18) C**
To become cheaper, the prices must round down. When rounded to the nearest 10p, 93p (tomatoes) becomes 90p and 84p (cabbage) becomes 80p, so these two items are now cheaper.

**19) 1270 cm**
1265 is halfway between 1260 and 1270.
1265 is equal to 1265, so 1265 cm rounds up to 1270 cm.

**20) 160 g**
159.50 is halfway between 159 and 160. 159.53 is more than 159.50, so 159.53 g rounds up to 160 g.

**21) B**
145 is halfway between 140 and 150. 147.5 is more than 145, so Josie's height rounds up to 150 cm. 145.3 is more than 145, so Martina's height also rounds up to 150 cm. This means that Martina and Josie have the same rounded height.

**22) B**
5500 is halfway between 5000 and 6000. 5495 is less than 5500, so 5495 rounds down to 5000. The population of Thelston is 6000, so 5495 can't be the answer.

**23) 78.5 kg**
78.45 is halfway between 78.4 and 78.5. 78.49 is more than 78.45, so 78.49 kg rounds up to 78.5 kg.

**24) E**
645 is halfway between 640 and 650.
646.1 is more than 645, so 646.1 rounds up to 650.

## Pages 6-7

**1) 0.2**
Start by finding the option with the lowest number of units. Both 0.2 and 0.7 have no units. Compare the digit in the tenths column. 2 is less than 7 so 0.2 is the lower number.

**2) −6**
The biggest negative number will have the lowest value. It will be the furthest number to the left on a number line. So −6 is a lower number than −2.

> means 'is greater than' and < means 'is less than'.
The correct symbol should be added to show whether the number on the left is greater than or smaller than the number on the right.

**3) >**   **4) >**   **5) <**

**6) B**
60 is written as 50 + 10 in Roman numerals, so it's LX.
4 is 5 − 1, which is written as IV in Roman numerals.
So together 64 is LXIV.

**7) 5 °C**
The lowest temperature is −3 °C on Monday and the highest temperature is 2 °C on Wednesday. The difference between −3 °C and 0 °C is 3 °C, and the difference between 0 °C and 2 °C is 2 °C. So, the total difference is 3 °C + 2 °C = 5 °C.

**8) E**
19 − 9 = 10, which is an even number.

**9) −48**
2 less than −26 is −28, and 20 less than −28 is −48.

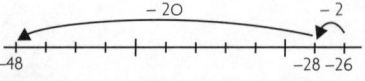

**10) 4**
4 should not be in the right-hand section of the Venn diagram. This section is for numbers that are greater than 5.

**11) 2**
2 is the only even number that is greater than −3.
1, 7 and 5 are all odd numbers, and −6 is less than −3.

**12) 24**
The first three multiples of 4 are 4, 8 and 12.
So Rabin's age is 4 + 8 + 12 = 24.

**13) E**
8 × 6 = 48 and 4 × 12 = 48. 48 is not divisible by 9, so 9 is not a factor.

**14) C**
3 × 6 = 18 and 2 × 9 = 18. So 18 is a multiple of both 6 and 9.

**15) 25**
The odd numbers that are between 0 and 10 are 1, 3, 5, 7 and 9. The sum of these numbers is 1 + 3 + 5 + 7 + 9 = 25.

**16) E**
The number of children in each team needs to be a factor of 36 to have equal teams. 8 is not a factor of 36, so you can't have equal teams of 8.

**17) E**
All of the multiples of 4 are even numbers (e.g. 4, 8, 12, 16 etc.) so Dolly is correct. Some multiples of three are even (e.g. 6, 12, 18, 24 etc.) so Cathy is incorrect. Not all multiples of 2 are also multiples of 4 (e.g. 2, 6, 10, 14 etc. are multiples of 2 but not 4), so Ellie is incorrect.

**18) D**
3, 5 and 6 are all factors of 30.
(10 × 3 = 30 and 5 × 6 = 30).
7, 4 and 8 are not factors of 30.

**19) 16, 20, 25**
16 is a multiple of 2: 8 × 2 = 16.
20 is a multiple of 2 and 5: 10 × 2 = 20 and 4 × 5 = 20.
25 is a multiple of 5: 5 × 5 = 25.

Answers

## Pages 8-9

To find the rule in a sequence, try to find how to get from one number to another. It can help to look at the difference between the numbers, or try to spot a pattern, e.g. the numbers double each time.

**1) 19**
The rule of the sequence is add 3.
**2) 30**
The rule of the sequence is add 6.
**3) 20**
The rule of the sequence is subtract 2.
**4) 10.5**
The rule of the sequence is add 0.5.
**5) 16**
The rule of the sequence is double the last number.
**6) 8**
The sequence is 2, 5, 8...
**7) 20**
The sequence is 8, 14, 20...
**8) 1**
The sequence is 0, 0.5, 1...
**9) 8**
The sequence is 20, 14, 8...
**10) 26**
The sequence is 36, 31, 26...
**11) 20**
The rule of the sequence is add 5. The term before the missing number is 15. 15 + 5 = 20
**12) 25**
The rule of the sequence is add 4. The term before the missing number is 21. 21 + 4 = 25
**13) 54**
The rule of the sequence is add 2. The term before the missing number is 52. 52 + 2 = 54
**14) 39**
The rule of the sequence is subtract 3. The term before the missing number is 42. 42 − 3 = 39
**15) 49**
The rule of the sequence is subtract 7. So, add 7 to 42 to find the missing number, 42 + 7 = 49.
**16) C**
Count on in 6s from 18 until you reach one of the given numbers: 18, 24, 30, 36...
**17) 6**
In each row there is one more tile than in the previous row, so in the 4th row there will be 3 + 1 = 4 tiles. In the 5th row there will be 4 + 1 = 5 tiles. In the 6th row there will be 5 + 1 = 6 tiles.
**18) 3**
Count back in 3s from 16: 16, 13, 10, 7, 4, 1... 3 is the only option that's not in the sequence.
**19) 17.5**
Count on in steps of 2.5 from 10: 10, 12.5, 15, 17.5...
**20) E**
Count back in 5s from 7: 7, 2, −3, −8...
**21) 21**
The 6th number in Jesper's sequence is 5 + 8 = 13, so the 7th number will be 8 + 13 = 21.
**22) A**
Count on in 5s from 2: 2, 7, 12, 17, 22, 27...
**23) D**
Gina plants 3 more seeds in each pot than she planted in the pot before. She plants 7 seeds in the 3rd pot, so she'll plant 7 + 3 = 10 seeds in the 4th pot and 10 + 3 = 13 seeds in the 5th pot.

## Page 10

To find what fraction of each shape is shaded, count up the total number of sections — this will be the denominator (bottom number) of the fraction. Then count the number of shaded sections — this will be the numerator (top number) of the fraction.

**1) E**   **2) C**   **3) B**
**4) D**   **5) A**
**6) 4**
Lakshmi eats ¼ of 16 sweets. ¼ of 16 is the same as 16 ÷ 4 = 4.
**7) B**
There are 12 squares in total and 5 of the squares are shaded. As a fraction this is 5/12.
**8) D**
The number line has been split into quarters with points at ¼, 2/4 and ¾. Arrow D is pointing at ¾.
**9) 20p**
You need to find ⅓ of 60p.
⅓ of 60p is the same as 60 ÷ 3 = 20p.
**10) B**
The fraction of the circle that is shaded is ¼.
The fraction of circle B that is shaded is 2/8.
These two fractions are equal (see the diagrams).

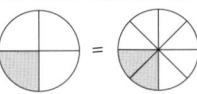

## Page 11

Make sure you know common fractions as decimals: ¼ = 0.25, ½ = 0.5, ¾ = 0.75. If the fraction is out of 10, then you need to put the numerator in the tenths column to make the decimal. For example, 2/10 is 0.2.

**1) 0.5**   **2) 0.25**   **3) 0.1**
**4) 0.75**   **5) 0.8**

For questions 6-8, convert the fractions to decimals and find the largest value in each row.

**6) 0.8**
½ = 0.5 and ¼ = 0.25. The values are 0.8, 0.5, 0.2, 0.75 and 0.25, so 0.8 is largest.
**7) ¾**
6/10 = 0.6, ¾ = 0.75 and ½ = 0.5. The values are 0.6, 0.75, 0.5, 0.4 and 0.5, so 0.75 (¾) is the largest.
**8) ¼**
¼ = 0.25, 1/10 = 0.1 and 2/10 = 0.2. The values are 0.25, 0.2, 0.1, 0.1 and 0.2, so 0.25 (¼) is the largest.
**9) 0.7**
7/10 means 7 tenths. Put 7 in the tenths column to make 0.7.
**10) ½**
Elizabeth got £0.50, which is half of £1.00, £0.50 × 2 = £1.00.
**11) E**
The total amount of pizza eaten by Micah and Rose is 2/4 + ¼ = ¾. This means that there is ¼ of the pizza left over. ¼ is 0.25 as a decimal.
**12) Susan**
3/10 means 3 tenths. Put 3 in the tenths column to make 0.3. Susan ate this amount of the cake.
**13) 3**
¼ = 0.25. ¾ = 0.75.
¼ + ¼ + ¼ = ¾ so there are three quarters in 0.75.

# Section Two — Working with Numbers

## Pages 12-13

You can add numbers using partitioning — breaking up one number into units, tens, hundreds, etc. and adding each of the parts to the other number, one at a time. It's usually easier to partition the smaller of the two numbers you're adding. You can also use a different written method such as the column method.

1) 42
33 + 9 = 42.

2) 70
23 splits into 20 + 3. 47 + 3 = 50, 50 + 20 = 70.

3) 101
16 splits into 10 + 6. 85 + 6 = 91, 91 + 10 = 101.

4) 113
48 splits into 40 + 8. 65 + 8 = 73, 73 + 40 = 113.

5) 265
54 splits into 50 + 4. 211 + 4 = 215, 215 + 50 = 265.

6) 378
38 splits into 30 + 8. 340 + 8 = 348, 348 + 30 = 378.

7) 704
19 splits into 10 + 9. 685 + 9 = 694, 694 + 10 = 704.

8) 689
182 splits into 100 + 80 + 2. 507 + 2 = 509, 509 + 80 = 589, 589 + 100 = 689.

9) £24.70
A jacket costs £22.50 and a hat costs £2.20, so find £22.50 + £2.20. £2.20 splits into £2.00 + £0.20. £22.50 + £0.20 = £22.70, £22.70 + £2.00 = £24.70.

10) £22.90
A scarf costs £7.40 and a jumper costs £15.50, so find £7.40 + £15.50. £7.40 splits into £7.00 + £0.40. £15.50 + £0.40 = £15.90, £15.90 + £7.00 = £22.90.

11) £29.90
A scarf costs £7.40 and a jacket costs £22.50, so find £7.40 + £22.50. £7.40 splits into £7.00 + £0.40. £22.50 + £0.40 = £22.90, £22.90 + £7.00 = £29.90.

12) £19.70
A shirt costs £12.30 and a scarf costs £7.40, so find £12.30 + £7.40. £7.40 splits into £7.00 + £0.40. £12.30 + £0.40 = £12.70, £12.70 + £7.00 = £19.70.

13) £27.80
A jumper costs £15.50 and a shirt costs £12.30, so find £15.50 + £12.30. £12.30 splits into £10.00 + £2.00 + £0.30. £15.50 + £0.30 = £15.80, £15.80 + £2.00 = £17.80, £17.80 + £10.00 = £27.80.

14) 91
45 splits into 40 + 5. 46 + 5 = 51, 51 + 40 = 91.

15) 766 g
320 splits into 300 + 20. 446 + 20 = 466, 466 + 300 = 766 g.

16) 665 g
315 splits into 300 + 10 + 5. 350 + 5 = 355, 355 + 10 = 365, 365 + 300 = 665 g.

17) 460 cm
133 splits into 100 + 30 + 3. 327 + 3 = 330, 330 + 30 = 360, 360 + 100 = 460 cm.

18) 377
Round 199 up to 200 by adding 1. Then do the calculation 200 + 178 = 378. To get the answer, you then just have to subtract the 1 you added to 199 at the beginning. 378 − 1 = 377.

19) 39
The total of all of the numbers is: 4 + 5 + 6 + 7 + 8 + 9 = 39.

20) 407
191 splits into 100 + 90 + 1. 216 + 1 = 217, 217 + 90 = 307, 307 + 100 = 407.

21) C
33 splits into 30 + 3. 57 + 3 = 60, 60 + 30 = 90.

22) 299 s
147 splits into 100 + 40 + 7. 152 + 7 = 159, 159 + 40 = 199, 199 + 100 = 299 seconds.

23) B
336 splits into 300 + 30 + 6. 582 + 6 = 588, 588 + 30 = 618, 618 + 300 = 918.

24) £3.71
Fish costs £2.46 and chips cost £1.25, so find £2.46 + £1.25. £1.25 splits into £1.00 + £0.20 + £0.05. £2.46 + £0.05 = £2.51, £2.51 + £0.20 = £2.71, £2.71 + £1.00 = £3.71.

25) 222
25 splits into 20 + 5. 85 + 5 = 90, 90 + 20 = 110.
54 splits into 50 + 4. 58 + 4 = 62, 62 + 50 = 112.
Add 110 and 112 to find the total. 110 splits into 100 + 10. 112 + 10 = 122, 122 + 100 = 222.

## Pages 14-15

You could use partitioning to find the answers to these subtractions. Break up the smaller number into units, tens, hundreds, etc. and subtract each of the parts from the other number, one at a time. You can also use a different written method such as the column method.

1) 61
12 splits into 10 + 2. 73 − 2 = 71, 71 − 10 = 61.

2) 35
34 splits into 30 + 4. 69 − 4 = 65, 65 − 30 = 35.

3) 53
47 splits into 40 + 7. 100 − 7 = 93, 93 − 40 = 53.

4) 48
77 splits into 70 + 7. 125 − 7 = 118, 118 − 70 = 48.

5) 126
72 splits into 70 + 2. 198 − 2 = 196, 196 − 70 = 126.

6) 24
225 splits into 200 + 20 + 5. 249 − 5 = 244, 244 − 20 = 224, 224 − 200 = 24.

7) 87
36 splits into 30 + 6. 123 − 6 = 117, 117 − 30 = 87.

8) 121
45 splits into 40 + 5. 166 − 5 = 161, 161 − 40 = 121.

9) 49
22 splits into 20 + 2. 71 − 2 = 69, 69 − 20 = 49.

10) 22p
Count back from £1 to 78p to find the difference between them. £1 − 20p = 80p, 80p − 2p = 78p. 20p + 2p = 22p.

11) £1.50
Count back from £5 to £3.50 to find the difference between them. £5 − £1 = £4, £4 − 50p = £3.50. £1 + 50p = £1.50.

12) £2.40
Count back from £5 to £2.60 to find the difference between them. £5 − £2 = £3, £3 − 40p = £2.60. £2 + 40p = £2.40.

13) £5.70
Count back from £10 to £4.30 to find the difference between them. £10 − £5 = £5, £5 − 70p = £4.30. £5 + 70p = £5.70.

Answers

**14) £2.15**
Count back from £10 to £7.85 to find the difference between them.  £10 − £2 = £8, £8 − 10p = £7.90, £7.90 − 5p = £7.85.  £2 + 10p + 5p = £2.15.
**15) 116**
16 splits into 10 + 6.  132 − 6 = 126, 126 − 10 = 116.
**16) D**
48 splits into 40 + 8.  71 − 8 = 63, 63 − 40 = 23.
**17) 122 litres**
You need to work out 167 − 45.  45 splits into 40 + 5.
167 − 5 = 162, 162 − 40 = 122.
**18) 128 cm**
172 splits into 100 + 70 + 2.  300 − 2 = 298,
298 − 70 = 228, 228 − 100 = 128 cm.
**19) 167**
Find the difference between the number of women and men at the gym.  You could split 98 into 90 + 8 and subtract these numbers separately.  265 − 8 = 257, 257 − 90 = 167.
Or you could say 98 = 100 − 2, so subtracting 98 is the same as subtracting 100 then adding 2.
265 − 100 = 165, 165 + 2 = 167.
**20) B**
136 splits into 100 + 30 + 6.  387 − 6 = 381,
381 − 30 = 351, 351 − 100 = 251.
**21) C**
The tallest sunflower is 213 cm and the shortest sunflower is 163 cm, so you need to work out 213 − 163.  One way to do this would be to count back from 213 to 163.

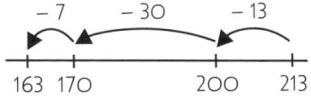

13 + 30 + 7 = 50 cm.
**22) D**
Count back from £10 to £6.65 to find the difference between them.  £10 − £3 = £7, £7 − 30p = £6.70,
£6.70 − 5p = £6.65.  £3 + 30p + 5p = £3.35.
**23) B**
38 splits into 30 + 8.  317 − 8 = 309, 309 − 30 = 279.

## Page 16

When you multiply by 10, move the digits one place to the left.  When you multiply by 100, move the digits two places to the left.  (Use zeros to fill any places to the left of the decimal point which are left empty.)  When you're dividing by 10 or 100, you move the digits the same number of places, but to the right.

**1) 700**
Move 70 one place to the left.
**2) 620**
Move 62 one place to the left.
**3) 2800**
Move 28 two places to the left.
**4) 51**
Move 510 one place to the right.
**5) 60**
Move 6000 two places to the right.
**6) 150**
The chickens lay 15 eggs in one day, so after 10 days they lay 15 × 10 eggs.  Move 15 one place to the left to give 150.
**7) 720p**
A packet of crisps costs 72p, so the box costs 10 × 72p.
Move 72 one place to the left to give 720p.

**8) B**
Divide the total amount by the cost of each ticket to find out how many tickets were sold, 6210 ÷ 10.  Move 6210 one place to the right to give 621.
**9) D**
The length of each piece is 500 ÷ 10.
Move 500 one place to the right to give 50 cm.
**10) D**
When you divide 440 by 10, you move
440 one place to the right to give 44.

## Pages 17-18

Use your 4, 5, 6 and 7 times tables to help you answer questions 1-5.
**1) £25**
5 × £5 = £25
**2) £28**
4 × £7 = £28
**3) £36**
6 × £6 = £36
**4) £32**
8 × £4 = £32
**5) £63**
9 × £7 = £63
**6) 120**
3 × 4 = 12.  30 is ten times larger than 3, so the answer will be ten times larger: 12 × 10 = 120.
**7) 450**
9 × 5 = 45.  90 is ten times larger than 9, so the answer will be ten times larger: 45 × 10 = 450.
**8) 420**
6 × 7 = 42.  70 is ten times larger than 7, so the answer will be ten times larger: 42 × 10 = 420.
**9) 180**
6 × 3 = 18.  60 is ten times larger than 6, so the answer will be ten times larger: 60 × 3 = 180.
**10) 400**
8 × 5 = 40.  80 is ten times larger than 8, so the answer will be ten times larger: 40 × 10 = 400.

You could use partitioning to find the answer to questions 11 to 15.  Break up one number into units, tens, hundreds, etc. and multiply each of the parts with the other number, one at a time — then add them together.  Or you could use a written method.
**11) 90**
15 splits into 10 + 5.  10 × 6 = 60, 5 × 6 = 30.
60 + 30 = 90.
**12) 81**
27 splits into 20 + 7.  20 × 3 = 60, 7 × 3 = 21.  60 + 21 = 81.
**13) 215**
43 splits into 40 + 3.  40 × 5 = 200, 3 × 5 = 15.
200 + 15 = 215.
**14) 144**
36 splits into 30 + 6.  30 × 4 = 120, 6 × 4 = 24.
120 + 24 = 144.
**15) 225**
45 splits into 40 + 5.  40 × 5 = 200, 5 × 5 = 25.
200 + 25 = 225.
**16) 4**
Use the nine times table to work out the missing number.
4 × 9 = 36.  Or you can use division to find the answer,
36 ÷ 9 = 4.

Answers

**17) 48**
The number of stickers Ross buys is the number of stickers in each pack multiplied by the number of packs.  6 × 8 = 48.
**18) 35 m**
You can find the length of the roll of ribbon by multiplying the length of each part by the number of parts.  5 m × 7 = 35 m.
**19) 270**
3 × 9 = 27.  30 is ten times larger than 3, so the answer will be 10 times larger.  27 × 10 = 270.
**20) A**
6 × 7 = 42 so option A is correct.
**21) C**
Round up 99p to £1.  3 × £1 = £3.  You added an extra 1p to the cost of each DVD, so in total you added 3 × 1p = 3p extra.  So the total cost of the DVDs is £3 − 3p = £2.97.
**22) A**
3 × 7 = 21.  30 is ten times larger than 3, so the answer will be ten times larger: 21 × 10 = 210.
**23) 184 km**
23 splits into 20 + 3.  20 × 8 = 160, 3 × 8 = 24.  160 + 24 = 184 km.
**24) B**
33 splits into 30 + 3.  30 × 4 = 120, 3 × 4 = 12.  120 + 12 = 132 people.

## Pages 19-20

**1) 8**
8 × 2 = 16, so 16 ÷ 2 = 8.
**2) 9**
9 × 3 = 27, so 27 ÷ 3 = 9.
**3) 7**
7 × 6 = 42, so 42 ÷ 6 = 7.
**4) 6**
6 × 6 = 36, so 36 ÷ 6 = 6.
**5) 9**
9 × 9 = 81, so 81 ÷ 9 = 9.

You could use partitioning to find the answer to more difficult division problems.  Break up the number you're dividing into more easily divisible parts and divide each of the parts separately.

**6) 1**
18 ÷ 2 = 9.  19 is 18 + 1, so 19 ÷ 2 = 9 r 1.
**7) 4**
42 ÷ 6 = 7.  46 = 42 + 4, so 46 ÷ 6 = 7 r 4.
**8) 6**
63 ÷ 9 = 7.  69 = 63 + 6, so 69 ÷ 7 = 7 r 6.
**9) 3**
You can split 68 into 50 + 18.  50 ÷ 5 = 10, 18 ÷ 5 = 3 r 3.  10 + 3 r 3 = 13 r 3.
**10) 4**
You can split 88 into 70 + 18.  70 ÷ 7 = 10, 18 ÷ 7 = 2 r 4.  10 + 2 r 4 = 12 r 4.
**11) £4**
4 × 4 = 16 so £16 ÷ 4 = £4.
**12) £15**
You can split £75 into £50 + £25.  £50 ÷ 5 = £10, £25 ÷ 5 = £5.  £10 + £5 = £15.

**13) £16**
You can split £96 into £60 + £36.  £60 ÷ 6 = £10, £36 ÷ 6 = £6.  £10 + £6 = £16.
**14) £32**
You can split £128 into £100 + £28.  £100 ÷ 4 = £25, £28 ÷ 4 = £7.  £25 + £7 = £32.
**15) £19**
You can split £57 into £30 + £27.  £30 ÷ 3 = £10, £27 ÷ 3 = £9.  £10 + £9 = £19.
**16) 23**
You can split 69 into 30 + 30 + 9.  30 ÷ 3 = 10, 30 ÷ 3 = 10, 9 ÷ 3 = 3.  10 + 10 + 3 = 23 books.
**17) B**
You can split 96 into 80 + 16.  80 ÷ 8 = 10, 16 ÷ 8 = 2.  10 + 2 = 12 books.
**18) 2**
You can split 86 into 60 + 26.  60 ÷ 6 = 10, 26 ÷ 6 = 4 r 2.  10 + 4 r 2 = 14 r 2.  There is a remainder of 2 so there are 2 eggs left over.
**19) C**
8 × 7 = 56 so 56 ÷ 7 = 8.
58 ÷ 7 = 8 r 2 so option C is incorrect.
**20) D**
You can split 60 into 40 + 20.  40 ÷ 4 = 10, 20 ÷ 4 = 5.  10 + 5 = 15.  So, 60 ÷ 4 = 15.
**21) 7**
Find the number in the 9 times table that's nearest to 68, and is also less than 68.  9 × 7 = 63, so 63 ÷ 9 = 7.  68 is 5 more than 63, so 68 ÷ 9 = 7 r 5.  So 7 is the number that should go into the box.
**22) 12**
Find the number in the 7 times table that's nearest to 79, and is also less than 79.  7 × 11 = 77, so 77 ÷ 7 = 11.  79 is 2 more than 77, so 79 ÷ 7 = 11 r 2.
Phoebe has enough coins to fill 11 complete pages with 2 coins left over.  So she will need 1 more page.  11 + 1 = 12 pages in total.
**23) C**
June divides 39 brownies between 4 boxes, so you need to work out 39 ÷ 4.  Find the number in the 4 times table that's nearest to 39, and is also less than 39.  4 × 9 = 36, so 36 ÷ 4 = 9.  39 is 3 more than 36, so 39 ÷ 4 = 9 r 3.  There is a remainder of 3, so June has 3 brownies left over.

# Section Three — Word Problems

## Pages 21-22

**1) £1**
Subtract the cost of the banana milkshake from the total cost to find the cost of the 2 mugs of hot chocolate: £2.50 − 50p = £2. The cost of each mug of hot chocolate is £2 ÷ 2 = £1.

**2) 1280**
Multiply the number of boxes by the number of sweets in each box to find the total number of sweets: 10 × 128 = 1280 fizzy sweets.

**3) 44p**
The cost of 4 chews is 4 × 8p = 32p. The cost of 1 chocolate mouse is 12p. So the total cost is 32p + 12p = 44p.

**4) £3**
Waleed was given £2 change, so the total cost of the 6 tickets is £20 − £2 = £18. Divide the total cost by the number of tickets to find the cost of each ticket: £18 ÷ 6 = £3.

**5) A**
Jodie has £20 and she needs to save another £20 (£40 − £20 = £20) to buy the jacket. She saves £4 each week, so the number of weeks that it will take her to save £20 is 20 ÷ 4 = 5 weeks.

**6) A**
To find the number Callum started with you need to work backwards from 6. He divided his number by 4, so do the opposite and multiply his answer by 4 to find the starting number: 6 × 4 = 24.

**7) C**
The cost of 2 scarves is 2 × £1.50 = £3. The cost of 1 bottle of perfume is £7. So the total cost is £3 + £7 = £10.

**8) B**
Nicola's dad's age is a multiple of 6. The only option that is a multiple of 6 is B — 6 × 6 = 36.

**9) £9**
Mr Bracken paid £15 for 10 litres of fuel so the cost of 1 litre is £15 ÷ 10 = £1.50. He used 6 litres to get to his aunt's house, so the cost of the journey is £1.50 × 6 = £9.

**10) A**
Compare the numbers that Robin and Arjen used to multiply and divide with. 4 is half of 8 and 3 is half of 6, so these numbers would give the same answer as Robin's calculation.
Or, you could choose a starting number and test each of the options until you find one that gives the same answer as Robin's calculation. Robin's calculation starting with 3:
3 × 8 = 24. 24 ÷ 6 = 4. Option A: 3 × 4 = 12. 12 ÷ 3 = 4.

**11) 15 m**
9 rabbit costumes is three times as many as 3 rabbit costumes, and 6 squirrel costumes is three times as many as 2 squirrel costumes. So, if Mrs Price can make 3 rabbit costumes and 2 squirrel costumes with 5 m of fabric, she needs 5 m × 3 = 15 m of fabric to make 9 rabbit costumes and 6 squirrel costumes.

**12) 500 g**
To make pasta carbonara for 4 people you use 400 g of pasta, so the amount of pasta for each person is 400 g ÷ 4 = 100 g. So, to make pasta carbonara for 5 people you need 5 × 100 g = 500 g.

**13) £5**
Yolanda uses two £15 vouchers to buy the books so the total cost of the books is 2 × £15 = £30. The 6 books are all the same price, so the cost of each book is £30 ÷ 6 = £5.

**14) D**
Divide the height of the stack by the height of each pack of butter to find the number of packs of butter in the stack:
12 ÷ 4 = 3 packs of butter. Each pack of butter weighs 200 g, so 3 packs would weigh 3 × 200 g = 600 g.

**15) 6**
The cost of 6 hair clips is £1.50 × 6 = £9. This means that Martha has £10 − £9 = £1 left over, which is not enough to buy another hair clip.

# Section Four — Data Handling

## Pages 23-24

For questions 1-5 you need to carefully read the data from the table.

**1) 3**  **2) Jumper**  **3) Blazer**
**4) Shorts**  **5) 8**

**6) 8**
Find the column for 2 pets and read down to find the number of people, 8.

**7) E**
The number of shops in Herdnell and Nolanbeck is 112 and the number of parks is 4.

**8) 31**
Add together the number of boys and girls in Year 5 to find the total number of children: 17 + 14 = 31.

**9) B**
Look at the difference between each pair of values in the table. The temperature fell from 39 °C at 12:30 to 34 °C at 13:00.
39 °C − 34 °C = 5 °C.

**10) B**
There are 40 children in total and 8 travel to school by car. So the number who did not travel by car is 40 − 8 = 32.

**11) 7**
Onions cost 20p each and Mrs Chung spent £1.40 on onions in total. £1.40 ÷ 7 = 20p. So Mrs Chung bought 7 onions.

**12) 5**
To find the number of girls who scored between 61 and 80 marks, subtract the number of girls who scored each set of marks from the total number of girls (20): 20 − 1 − 4 − 8 − 2 = 5.

**13) 7**
There were 26 doughnuts sold in total and 10 were sold in the afternoon, so 26 − 10 = 16 doughnuts were sold in the morning. To find the number of brownies sold in the morning, subtract the number of doughnuts and cookies sold in the morning from the total number of items sold in the morning: 30 − 16 − 7 = 7.

## Pages 25-26

**1) Thursday**
The day when the most tomatoes were picked will have the tallest bar — Thursday.

**2) Friday**
Find 10 on the vertical axis and read across until you find a bar which is exactly at 10. Mr Potter picked 10 tomatoes on Friday.

**3) 11**
Look at the top of the bar for Monday and read across to the vertical axis. Mr Potter picked 11 tomatoes on Monday.

**4) 32**
Mr Potter picked 22 tomatoes on Thursday and 10 tomatoes on Friday. 22 + 10 = 32 tomatoes.

**5) E**
Each symbol on the pictogram shows 4 buttons. There are 2½ symbols for red buttons. ½ of 4 is 2, 2 × 4 = 8. 2 + 8 = 10 red buttons in total.

**6) March**
Each square up the vertical axis is worth 100 ice creams, so if you count up 3 squares on the vertical axis you'll reach 300. Read across from 300 to find the month which is exactly at 300 — March.

**7) 9**
Each symbol on the pictogram shows 6 birds. There are 3 symbols for ducks, so she saw 3 × 6 = 18 ducks. There are 1½ symbols for turkeys. ½ of 6 is 3, 1 × 6 = 6. So she saw 3 + 6 = 9 turkeys in total. To find the difference you subtract the number of turkeys from the number of ducks: 18 − 9 = 9. (Or you could work out that there are 1½ more symbols for ducks than turkeys on the pictogram. 1 symbol = 6, ½ a symbol = 6 ÷ 2 = 3 — so she saw 6 + 3 = 9 more ducks than turkeys.)

**8) 90 minutes**
Read off the values for each day from the chart. Then add them all together to find the total. 20 (Monday) + 15 (Tuesday) + 10 (Wednesday) + 15 (Thursday) + 30 (Friday) = 90 minutes.

**9) 36**
Each symbol on the pictogram shows 8 matches. There are 3 symbols for 2 goals, so 2 goals were scored in 3 × 8 = 24 matches. There are 1½ symbols for 3 goals. ½ of 8 is 4 and 1 × 8 = 8. So 3 goals were scored in 4 + 8 = 12 matches. To find the total number of matches in which they scored 2 or more goals you add them together: 24 + 12 = 36 matches.

**10) D**
The graph shows that 4 children play 251-300 minutes of sport each week, so option D is true.

**11) 6**
5 people voted for ready salted, 8 people voted for cheese and onion and 7 people voted for salt and vinegar. The total who voted for these 3 flavours is 5 + 8 + 7 = 20 people. There were 26 people asked in total, so the number who voted for prawn cocktail is 26 − 20 = 6 people.

# Section Five — Shape and Space

## Page 27

Make sure you know what a 90° angle looks like. 90° is also called a right angle. A 180° angle is twice the size of a 90° angle (so it's the same as two right angles).

**1) C**

**2) D**
Angle D is smaller than 90°.

**3) B**

**4) A**
Angle A is larger than 90° but not as large as 180°.

**5) C**
There are 2 right angles in the shape.

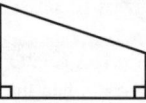

**6) 3**
The numbers 12 and 3 on a clock are at 90° to each other.

**7) C**
C is smaller than all of the other angles because the ends of the two lines that make up the angle are closest together in C.

**8) 2**
Josie turns through 1 right angle as she turns from south to west, and one right angle as she turns from west to north. So she turns through 2 right angles in total.

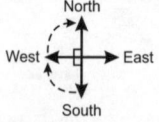

**9) 45°**
Angle a is smaller than a right angle. 45° is the only option that is smaller than 90°, so this is the size of a.

## Page 28

**1) B**
A pentagon has 5 sides and 5 corners — so it's shape B.

**2) D**
A circle has no corners — so it's shape D.

**3) E**
An equilateral triangle has 3 equal sides and 3 equal angles — so it's shape E.

**4) A**
An isosceles triangle has only 2 equal sides — so it's shape A.

**5) C**
A square has 4 equal sides and 4 right angles — so it's shape C.

**6) A**
An equilateral triangle has 3 equal sides and 3 equal angles — so it's shape A.

**7) B**
A quadrilateral has 4 sides. Shape B has 5 sides so it is not a quadrilateral.

**8) E**

To go in the shaded box, the shape must have at least one right angle and sides that are the same length. A square has 4 right angles and all of its sides are equal in length. So it can be placed in the shaded box.

**9) C**

The angles in the right-angled triangle are not all equal. So C is the correct answer.

# Page 29

**1) 12 cm**

3 + 3 + 3 + 3 = 12 cm

**2) B**

3 + 2 + 3 + 2 = 10 cm

**3) 12 cm²**

There are twelve 1 cm² squares inside shape D.

**4) 9 cm²**

There are nine 1 cm² squares inside shape C.

**5) 14 cm**

4 + 3 + 4 + 3 = 14 cm

**6) 24 cm**

Add up the length of the six sides to find the perimeter of the hexagon. 4 + 4 + 4 + 4 + 4 + 4 (or 6 × 4) = 24 cm.

**7) D**

Add up the length of every side of the shape to find its perimeter. 3 + 5 + 6 + 2 + 9 + 7 = 32 cm.

**8) 18 cm²**

Count the number of squares within the triangle to find its area. There are 15 full squares and 6 half squares. 2 half squares added together make 1 whole square, so the 6 half squares make up 3 full squares in total. So the area of the triangle is 15 + 3 = 18 cm².

**9) E**

The perimeter of the vegetable patch is found by adding up the four sides. The two longest sides are both 10 m, so the total length of the two shortest sides is 28 − 10 − 10 = 8 m.
The two short sides add up to 8 m, so the length of each side is 8 ÷ 2 = 4 m. So the width of the vegetable patch is 4 m.

# Page 30

A line of symmetry is a straight line that divides a shape into two parts that are reflections of each other.

**1) B**

Shape B has four lines of symmetry.

**2) D**

Shape D has one line of symmetry.

**3) E**

Shape E has three lines of symmetry.

**4) A**

Shape A has two lines of symmetry.

**5) C**

Shape C has five lines of symmetry.

**6) 2**

A rectangle has two lines of symmetry.

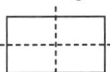

**7) N**

The letter 'N' has no lines of symmetry.

**8) D**

The diagram shows the reflection of the shape. This shape is option D.

**9) C**

Point X is 3 squares above the mirror line. So the reflection of X will be 3 squares below the mirror line. This is shown by C.

# Page 31

The thick and dotted lines show the shape's edges — this helps you to see the number of faces the shape has.

**1) B**    **2) A**    **3) E**

**4) C**    **5) D**

**6) C**

The net is made up of 6 square faces so it could only make a cube.

**7) E**

Shape E has 2 pentagonal faces and 5 rectangular faces. It is the only option that has 7 faces.

**8) D**

The net is made up of 4 triangles. It will fold up to make a triangle-based pyramid — option D is correct.

**9) C**

The shape in the middle section of the Venn diagram should have 1 or more curved faces and 1 or more triangular faces. A cuboid has neither curved faces nor triangular faces, so it should not be in the Venn diagram.

## Page 32

For questions 1-5, you need to count
the number of cubes in each shape.
1) A    2) C    3) B
4) E    5) D
6) C

Reflect the shape on the left in option C in a vertical mirror line. The two shapes then fit together to make shape X.

7) D

Option D shows the shape after it has been reflected.

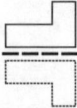

8) B

Shape W has been rotated 180° to give option B.

## Page 33

To find the coordinates of each object, read down from the object to find the letter. Then read across from the object to find the number.
1) B3    2) A2    3) E6
4) D1    5) F4
6) E

Read up from the letter B and across from the number 3 to find the square B3. Carlos has drawn a triangle in this square.

7) A

Read down from point B to find the *x*-coordinate (3)
and then across from point B to find the *y*-coordinate (7).
The coordinates of point B are (3, 7).

8) C

To go from A to B, you need to move A left and up. Count how many squares A needs to move — it moves three left and one up.

# Section Six — Units and Measures

## Page 34

1) **0.3 litres**

The only volumes are 0.3 litres and 5 ml.
5 ml is far too little liquid for a full mug of tea.

2) **7 cm**

The only lengths are 100 m and 7 cm.
100 m is far too long for a finger.

3) **100 g**

This is the only weight measurement.

4) **5 ml**

The only volumes are 0.3 litres and 5 ml.
0.3 litres is far too much liquid for a teaspoon.

5) **100 m**

The only lengths are 100 m and 7 cm.
7 cm is far too short for the length of a football pitch.

6) **275 ml**

There are 4 spaces between the 200 ml mark and the 300 ml mark.
So 4 spaces are equal to 300 ml − 200 ml = 100 ml.
1 space = 100 ml ÷ 4 = 25 ml. The liquid is 1 mark below the 300 ml line. So there is 25 ml less than 300 ml in the bottle:
300 ml − 25 ml = 275 ml.

7) **180 cm**

Mrs Patel bought 30 cm + 1.5 m of chain.
Make 1.5 m the same unit as 30 cm:
1 m = 100 cm, so 1.5 m = 1.5 × 100 = 150 cm
She bought 30 cm + 150 cm = 180 cm of chain in total.

8) **4**

1 litre = 1000 ml, 2 litres = 2 × 1000 ml = 2000 ml
Each bottle is 500 ml, 4 × 500 = 2000, so 4 bottles are needed to fill the jug.

9) **A**

Total weight of all the bags = 10 × 350 g = 3500 g.
1000 g = 1 kg, so 3500 g = 3500 ÷ 1000 = 3.5 kg.

10) **C**

There is 10 km − 9¾ km = ¼ km left. 1 km = 1000 m,
so ¼ km = ¼ of 1000 m = 250 m.

## Page 35

1) **A**

There are 60 minutes in an hour, so ten minutes to five o'clock is the same as 4:50.

2) **D**

Half past seven means half an hour past seven o'clock.
Half an hour is 30 minutes, so the digital time is 7:30.

3) **B**

Quarter to six means 15 minutes before six o'clock.
This is the same as 5:45.

4) **E**

Quarter to seven is the same as 6:45.
6:15 is half an hour (30 minutes) before 6:45.

5) **C**

Ten minutes to five is the same as 4:50. Add twenty minutes on: 10 minutes takes you to 5 o'clock. Another 10 minutes takes you to 5:10.

6) **B**

Read across the 'Hospital' row for the arrival times at the Hospital. The latest bus that Sarah can get arrives at 10:55. You're asked for the time that this bus leaves Whitdale, which is 10:30.

7) **3 weeks**

There are 31 days in May, and she's on holiday from the 24th day — this means there are 23 days in May that she's not on holiday for. So she is on holiday for 31 − 23 = 8 days in May. She is also on holiday for 13 days in June, so altogether she is away for 8 + 13 = 21 days. There are 7 days in a week, so the number of weeks she's on holiday for is 21 ÷ 7 = 3 weeks.

8) **7:55 pm**

1 hour = 60 minutes. So 70 minutes = 1 hour + 10 minutes.
1 hour later than 6:45 pm is 7:45 pm. 10 minutes later than 7:45 pm is 7:55 pm.

9) **2:35 pm**

It takes Mrs Brown 35 minutes to drive and 5 minutes to park, so you need to subtract these times from 3:15 pm.
Subtract 5 minutes from 3:15 pm to get to 3:10 pm.
Subtract 35 minutes from 3:10 pm to get to 2:35 pm.

10) **D**

To add on 11 hours, add on 12 hours then subtract 1 hour.
12 hours later than 10:15 am is 10:15 pm (remember, am is morning and pm is evening). Subtracting 1 hour gives 9:15 pm.

# Section Seven — Mixed Problems

## Page 36

**1) D**
Shape D has two pairs of sides which are equal in length and four right angles, so it could be placed in the shaded area of the Venn diagram.

**2) £45.00**
The total number of hours that Anna worked is
4½ + 5½ = 10 hours. She was paid £4.50 for each hour of work, so the amount of money she earns in total is:
10 × £4.50 = £45.00.

**3) £2.40**
There are 1000 ml in 1 litre. 2 × 500 ml = 1000 ml, or 1 litre.
One 500 ml bottle of water costs 40p, so 1 litre of water would cost 2 × 40p = 80p. So 3 litres of water costs
80p × 3 = 240p, or £2.40.

**4) C**
Three out of the five shapes have one line of symmetry. This is written as ⅗.

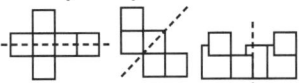

**5) E**
The amount of time it takes Hilda to wash all eight cars is
8 × 10 = 80 minutes, or 1 hour and 20 minutes. Count 1 hour and 20 minutes on from 4:45 pm. 1 hour on takes you to 5:45 pm and a further 20 minutes on takes you to 6:05 pm.

**6) 2000 m**
There are 60 minutes in an hour, so 15 minutes is ¼ of an hour (60 ÷ 4 = 15). So the distance Lucy runs in 15 minutes is 8 ÷ 4 = 2 km. There are 1000 m in 1 kilometre so to convert this into metres, multiply by 1000:
2 × 1000 = 2000 m.

**7) A**
The diagram shows the shape after it has been reflected.
Add up the length of every side to find the perimeter of the shape:
4 + 4 + 3 + 5 + 5 + 3 = 24 cm.

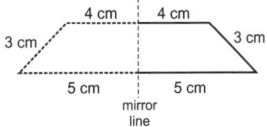

# Assessment Test 1

## Pages 37-41

**1) C**
You could add up the pounds and then add up the pence:
£2 + £1 = £3. 5p + 2p + 2p = 9p. Then add them together:
£3 + 9p = £3.09

**2) C**
This is the route taken:

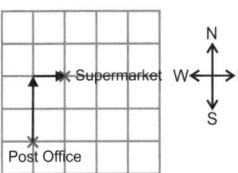

**3) E**
295 is half way between 300 and 290, so it rounds up to 300 when rounded to the nearest 10.

**4) B**
The key tells you that each symbol represents 2 plants, so half a symbol represents 1 plant. There are 2½ symbols on the pictogram for beans. 2 + 2 + 1 = 5 bean plants.

**5) D**
A line of symmetry passes through each of the 5 corners:

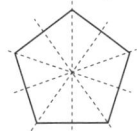

**6) D**
80 is ten times bigger than 8. So the answer to 7 × 80 will be 10 times bigger than 56. 56 × 10 = 560.

**7) 5**
Read the numbers of children off the vertical scale.
12 children go to art club, 7 children go to dance club.
12 − 7 = 5. 5 more children go to art club.

**8) B**
36 is in both the 6 times table and the 9 times table (6 × 6 = 36 and 4 × 9 = 36).
So 6 and 9 are both factors of 36.

**9) B**
A 90° angle is a right angle.
The only angle bigger than a right angle is B.

**10) B**
None of the numbers in the right-hand circle are multiples of 11, 7 or 6, or odd, but they are all even.
So the correct label must be "Even numbers".

**11) B**
You can find the difference between 998 and 1029 by counting up:

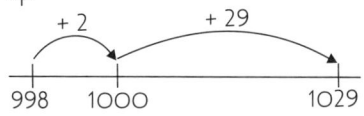

Add 2 to get to 1000, and then add 29 to get to 1029. 2 + 29 = 31

**12) 6**

Divide the total number of biscuits by the number of biscuits in each bag to get the number of bags.
48 ÷ 8 = 6 bags.

**13) A**

Area means the amount of space taken up by the shape. Count up the squares and half squares in the shape. There are 6 whole squares and 2 half squares. 2 half squares are the same as a whole square. Each square is 1 cm², so the area of the shape is 6 + 1 = 7 cm².

**14) Thursday**

A number line shows that −3 is lower than the other numbers in the table because it is furthest to the left.

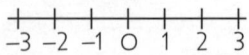

So −3 °C is the coldest temperature in the table.

**15) D**

XXX is 30, I is 1 and V is 5. I comes before the V so you have to subtract it: 5 − 1 = 4. Adding together you get 30 + 4 = 34.

**16) 344**

You can multiply 43 by 8 using partitioning. 43 splits into 40 + 3. Now multiply both parts by 8: 4 × 8 = 32. 40 is 10 times bigger than 4, so the answer will be 10 times bigger. 32 × 10 = 320. 3 × 8 = 24. Add them together: 320 + 24 = 344

**17) E**

Add the amounts for carbohydrate, 49 g, and fat, 2 g, together. 49 + 2 = 51 g.

**18) E**

An irregular shape has sides that are different lengths. All the shapes have sides the same length apart from E.

**19) C**

There are 10 gaps between 68 and 69. So each gap represents 1 tenth or 0.1. The arrow points to 5 gaps after 68, which is 68 + 0.5 = 68.5.

**20) 36p**

10 stamps cost £3.60, so 1 stamp will cost £3.60 ÷ 10. Divide by 10 by moving the digits one place to the right. So £3.60 ÷ 10 = £0.36 = 36p.

**21) C**

Think of a shape divided into 8 equal parts. ⅛ of this shape is 1 of these parts:

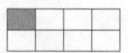

⅜ of this shape is 3 of the 8 parts, so ⅜ is bigger than ⅛. ¼ of this shape is 2 of the 8 parts, so ¼ is bigger than ⅛. ¾ is bigger than ¼, so ¾ is bigger than ⅛. ½ of this shape is 4 of the 8 parts, so ½ is bigger than ⅛. So ⅛ is the smallest fraction.

**22) 100 m**

The playground is a rectangle, so it has two sides of 20 m and two sides of 30 m. Adding the lengths of all the sides together gives you the perimeter:
20 m + 20 m + 30 m + 30 m = 100 m

**23) 3 weeks**

He gets £2.40 a week, so after 2 weeks he will have £2.40 + £2.40. Partition one lot of £2.40 into £2 + 40p and then add the numbers one at a time:
£2.40 + £2 = £4.40, £4.40 + 40p = £4.80.
After 3 weeks he will have: £4.80 + £2.40.
£4.80 + £2 = £6.80, £6.80 + 40p = £7.20, so after 3 weeks he will have saved £7.20.

**24) B**

Shape B has 5 faces: two triangular faces at the ends, and three rectangular faces in the middle. It also has 9 edges.

**25) B**

7 + 7 + 7 + 7 = 28. So 28 = ☐ × 2. 28 ÷ 2 = 14

**26) D**

Use a timeline to count along. She's cycling for 35 minutes and then takes a 15 minute break. Split the 35 minutes up into 30 minutes and 5 minutes, then add on the 15 minute break.

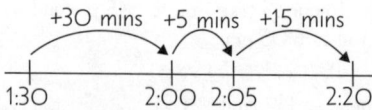

So Siti finishes her break at 2:20 pm.

**27) D**

Claire gives half of 80 stickers to Luke — so Luke gets 80 ÷ 2 = 40 stickers. Luke gives one quarter of his 40 stickers to Jenny — so Jenny gets 40 ÷ 4 = 10 stickers.

**28) D**

14 children have brown hair and 7 children have blonde hair. 14 − 7 = 7, so 7 more children have brown hair than blonde hair, not 8. So D is incorrect.

**29) E**

Convert the measurements into the same units:
1 m = 100 cm, so 2 m = 2 × 100 cm = 200 cm.
Total length of ribbon cut from the roll = 75 cm × 2 = 150 cm.
Length of ribbon left = 200 cm − 150 cm = 50 cm.
There are 100 cm in 1 m, so 50 cm = 50 ÷ 100 = 0.5 m.

**30) D**

Work backwards from 50. The last thing she does is add 1 to a number to get 50. So subtract 1 from 50 to find this number: 50 − 1 = 49. She multiplied her start number by 7 to get 49. So divide 49 by 7 to find her start number: 49 ÷ 7 = 7. So she started with 7.

# Assessment Test 2

## Pages 42-46

**1) D**
The 7 is in the thousands column, so it is worth seven thousand.

| Thousands | Hundreds | Tens | Units |
|---|---|---|---|
| 7 | 0 | 5 | 2 |

**2) A**
There are 4 edges around the top of the cube, 4 edges down the sides of the cube and 4 edges around the bottom of the cube. 4 + 4 + 4 = 12 edges.

**3) C**
72 is in the 8 times table, 9 × 8 = 72. So it must divide exactly by 8, 72 ÷ 8 = 9.

**4) C**
The highest bar shows the most popular type of dog — it is 'Beagle'. Read off the value on the vertical axis to find out how many children chose 'Beagle' — 11 children.

**5) B**
0.35, 0.98 and 0.65 are the smallest three numbers, because they have 0 units. 0.35 has three tenths, 0.98 has nine tenths and 0.65 has six tenths, so from smallest to largest the order is 0.35, 0.65, 0.98. 1.03 and 1.30 both have 1 unit, but 1.03 is smaller than 1.30 because it has 0 tenths whereas 1.30 has 3 tenths. So the order is 0.35, 0.65, 0.98, 1.03, 1.30.

**6) D**
An equilateral triangle has 3 equal sides and 3 equal angles.

**7) 2**
Turning from north to south means going through 2 right angles.

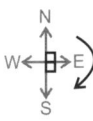

**8) C**
C is the only shape with a line of symmetry, which is shown below.

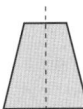

**9) E**
A week has 7 days, so if she visits her grandma on 12th February, she'll visit again on 12 + 7 = 19th February.

**10) B**
< means 'is less than'. So the number that goes in the box must be less than 4652. 4599 is less than 4652 because although they both have the same number of thousands, 4599 has a smaller number of hundreds.

**11) 1 °C**
Find the bar for Wednesday and read across to the vertical axis, the temperature was 2 °C. Find the bar for Saturday and read across to the vertical axis, the temperature was 3 °C. To find the difference in temperature subtract the lower temperature from the higher temperature: 3 °C − 2 °C = 1 °C.

**12) 323**
You're told that 60 − 37 = 23, so you just need to subtract the hundreds in 560 − 237 and add 23. 500 − 200 = 300. 300 + 23 = 323

**13) D**
To divide a number by 100 you move the digits two places to the right. 4500 ÷ 100 = 45.

**14) 5**
Each wheel symbol shows 4 vehicles. So each quarter of a wheel shows 4 ÷ 4 = 1 vehicle. Motorbikes: 2 quarters of a wheel = 2. Buses: 3 quarters of a wheel = 3. The total of motorbikes and buses is: 2 + 3 = 5.

**15) B**
In 5 packs there will be 5 × 6 = 30 apples, which isn't enough for 32 children. In 6 packs there will be 6 × 6 = 36 apples, which is enough for 32 children.

**16) £29**
£87 is divided equally between 3 people. So each person gets £87 ÷ 3. You can work this out by partitioning 87 into 60 + 27. Then divide each part by 3. 60 ÷ 3 = 20, 27 ÷ 3 = 9. So 87 ÷ 3 = 20 + 9 = 29. Each person gets £29.

**17) D**
5250 is halfway between 5200 and 5300. 5240 is less than 5250, so 5240 rounds down to 5200.

**18) D**
Find the difference between the numbers in the sequence to work out the rule. The difference between 13 and 9 is 13 − 9 = 4. The difference between 9 and 5 is 9 − 5 = 4, etc. So the rule of the sequence is subtract 4.

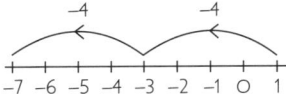

The next number in the sequence is −7.

**19) C**
12 out of the 16 small squares are shaded, which is 12/16, so 3/4 = 12/16.

**20) A**
The first coordinate (1) is the distance across the horizontal axis. The second coordinate (4) is the distance up the vertical axis. Going 1 unit across and 4 units up takes you to point A.

**21) C**
1 kg = 1000 g so 2 kg = 1000 g × 2 = 2000 g
½ kg = half of 1000 g, 1000 g ÷ 2 = 500 g
2½ kg = 2000 g + 500 g = 2500 g

**22) 18 m**
The trampoline is a regular hexagon, which has 6 equal sides. The perimeter is the distance around the edge of the shape. The sides are each 3 m long, so the perimeter = 3 × 6 = 18 m.

## 23) B
The squares gain an extra row and an extra column each time. The next square will have 4 + 1 = 5 rows and 4 + 1 = 5 columns of counters. To calculate the number of counters in the next square multiply 5 by 5 (5 rows of 5 counters). 5 × 5 = 25 counters.

## 24) E
Vikram's dog weighs 16 kg, which means it comes under the 'up to 30 kg' category. So the dog should have 4 biscuits a day. There are 7 days in a week, so Vikram's dog should have 4 × 7 = 28 biscuits per week.

## 25) C
Work out how long the party is: From 4 pm to 6 pm is 2 hours. From 6 pm to 6:30 pm is 30 minutes. So the party lasts for 2 hours 30 minutes. They have the cake halfway through the party and half of 2 hours 30 minutes is 1 hour 15 minutes. Count on 1 hour 15 minutes from the start time of 4:00 pm: 4:00 pm + 1 hour = 5:00 pm
5:00 pm + 15 minutes = 5:15 pm

## 26) £25.50
The children's tickets cost £3.50 × 3.
You can work this out by partitioning: £3.50 splits into £3 + 50p. £3 × 3 = £9, 50p × 3 = £1.50.
£9 + £1.50 = £10.50. The adults' tickets cost £7.50 × 2.
You can work this out by partitioning: £7.50 splits into £7 + 50p. £7 × 2 = £14, 50p × 2 = £1. £14 + £1 = £15
So the total cost for the whole family is:
£10.50 + £15 = £25.50

## 27) A
Area means the amount of space taken up by the shape.
To find the area of a rectangle, multiply the width by the length:
9 m × 6 m = 54 m².

## 28) B
6 packets of raisins weigh 6 × 65 g.
You can work this out by partitioning:
65 g splits into 60 g + 5 g.
6 × 60 g = 360 g, 6 × 5 g = 30 g.
360 g + 30 g = 390 g.
Round 390 g to the nearest 100 g:
350 is halfway between 300 and 400.
390 is more than 350, so 390 g rounds up to 400 g.

## 29) 8 days
1 litre = 1000 ml, so
2 litres = 2 × 1000 ml = 2000 ml.
The horse has 250 ml a day, so after 2 days it has had:
250 + 250 = 500 ml.
After 3 days: 500 + 250 = 750 ml
After 4 days: 750 + 250 = 1000 ml.
If 1000 ml lasts for 4 days, 2000 ml will last twice as long. So 2000 ml will last 2 × 4 days = 8 days.

## 30) C
£1.25 × 3 is £1.25 + £1.25 + £1.25 = £3.75
Now subtract £3.75 from £10.00.
You can do this by counting up from £3.75 to £10.00:
£3.75 + £0.25 = £4.00. £4.00 + £6.00 = £10.00
£0.25 + £6.00 = £6.25 change.

# Assessment Test 3
## Pages 47-51

### 1) B
The shape has 5 sides so it's a pentagon.

### 2) 3017
There are 3 thousands, so put 3 in the thousands column. There are no hundreds, so put zero in the hundreds column.
17 is one ten and 7 units:

| Thousands | Hundreds | Tens | Units |
|---|---|---|---|
| 3 | 0 | 1 | 7 |

### 3) B
30 children are split into teams of 5.
So the number of teams is 30 ÷ 5 = 6.

### 4) 14
To find the difference, you could count back from 73 to 59.
73 − 3 = 70
70 − 10 = 60
60 − 1 = 59
3 + 10 + 1 = 14

### 5) 5
Each symbol shows 2 animals, so half a symbol shows 1 animal. There are 2½ symbols for sheep, which shows 2 + 2 + 1 = 5 sheep.

### 6) A
There are 3 lines of symmetry:

### 7) Cricket
The sport that was chosen by fewest children has the shortest bar. This is cricket.

### 8) A
90 and 72 are both in the 9 times table, so they are both multiples of 9. (90 = 10 × 9, 72 = 8 × 9)

### 9) A
The hexagon is split into 6 equal sections. 1 section is shaded, which is ⅙ of the hexagon.

### 10) B
A right angle is 90° and angle y is smaller than a right angle. The only answer option that is smaller than 90° is 40°.

### 11) D
The arrow is pointing to the mark ¾ of the way from 0 to 1.
¾ is equivalent to 0.75. Alternatively, you can work it out by looking at the possible options. The point in the middle, halfway between 0 and 1, is ½ or 0.5. So the arrow is pointing to a number between 0.5 and 1. The only option which has a value between 0.5 and 1 is D, 0.75.

### 12) 2 °C
To find the temperature that is 3 °C warmer than the temperature shown on the thermometer (which is −1 °C), count up 3 °C.
This brings you to 2 °C.

### 13) 235p
In £1 there are 100 pence. So in £2 there are 100 × 2 = 200 pence. So in £2.35 there will be 200 + 35 = 235 pence.

### 14) A
Draw an arrow to the elephants from the giraffes. It will be pointing in the same direction as the SW arrow on the compass. So the elephants are south-west of the giraffes.

### 15) A
Twenty minutes to three means that it is twenty minutes before three o'clock. There are 60 minutes in an hour, so 'twenty minutes to' is the same as 60 − 20 = 40 minutes past the previous hour. So twenty minutes to three is the same as 2:40.

**16) 26 m**
The perimeter is the total distance around the edge of the shape, so add up the lengths of each side:
5 m + 3 m + 7 m + 7 m + 4 m = 26 m

**17) 5**
There is 1 square face for the base, and 4 triangular faces. This is 5 faces in total.

**18) 18 minutes**
The bus leaves Shipford at 8:28 am and gets to Uptown at 8:46 am. There are 2 minutes from 8:28 until 8:30. Then there are 16 minutes from 8:30 until 8:46. The bus takes 2 + 16 = 18 minutes in total.

**19) D**
Katy's number multiplied by 4 is 88.
So Katy's number will be 88 ÷ 4, because division is the opposite of multiplication. To do this calculation, partition 88 into 40 + 40 + 8, then divide each part by 4:
40 ÷ 4 = 10, 8 ÷ 4 = 2
So 88 ÷ 4 = 10 + 10 + 2 = 22.

**20) £38.40**
£1.50 more than £36.90 is £36.90 + £1.50.
Partition £1.50 into £1 + 50p and add each bit separately:
£36.90 + £1 = £37.90. £37.90 + 50p = £38.40

**21) D**
Count on in 4s from 3. 3, 7, 11, 15, 19

**22) 148**
37 × 4 can be worked out by partitioning 37 into 30 + 7 and multiplying each part by 4 separately: 30 × 4 = 120, 7 × 4 = 28. Now add the products together to get the answer: 120 + 28 = 148.

**23) E**
1 litre = 1000 ml. Each ice cube is 10 ml. So the number of ice cubes she can make is 1000 ÷ 10 = 100.

**24) 24**
⅓ of the path is made of 8 stones, so there will be three times as many stones in the whole path. 8 × 3 = 24 stones.

**25) C**
The juice is £1.49 and the cookie is 60p, so £1.49 + 60p = £2.09. To find the change from £5 you need to work out: £5 − £2.09. £2.09 can be partitioned into £2 + 9p. £5 − £2 = £3. £3 − 9p = £2.91.

**26) A**
485 is exactly halfway between 480 and 490, so 485 rounds up to 490. All the other options round up or down to 480.

**27) 1 and 2**
To find the area of a rectangle, you multiply the length by the width.
Area of rectangle 1 = 6 × 2 = 12 cm².
Area of rectangle 2 = 4 × 3 = 12 cm².

**28) E**
45 ml of olive oil is needed for 4 people. 12 people is 3 times as many as 4 people (4 × 3 = 12). So 3 × 45 ml of olive oil is needed. Partition 45 ml into 40 ml + 5 ml and multiply each part by 3 separately: 40 ml × 3 = 120 ml, 3 × 5 ml = 15 ml.
So, 3 × 45 ml = 120 ml + 15 ml = 135 ml.

**29) (2, 3)**
Read down from point A to the horizontal axis for the first coordinate (2). Then read across from point A to the vertical axis for the second coordinate (3). So A is at (2, 3).

**30) A**
The court is nine 80 cm strides wide.
So the width is 9 × 80 = 720 cm.
1 m = 100 cm, so 720 cm is 7 m 20 cm.
So the court is 7 m wide to the nearest metre.

# Assessment Test 4

## Pages 52-56

**1) C**
Hexagons have 6 sides, so shape C is the only possible answer.

**2) C**
An apple is easy to pick up and feels quite light, so 3 kg and 30 kg are too heavy. A feather weighs around 1 g, so 0.3 g and 3 g are much too light to be the weight of an apple. 0.3 kg is the correct answer.

**3) 0.47**
Look at the place value of the first number in each of the values given. 0.47 has no units and is the only number to have no values greater than tenths. So 0.47 is the smallest number.

**4) B**
Look for the answer option that all the numbers in the list are divisible by — 3 is the only possible answer. (18 ÷ 3 = 6, 30 ÷ 3 = 10, 15 ÷ 3 = 5, 12 ÷ 3 = 4, 36 ÷ 3 = 12.)

**5) A**
The even numbers between 1 and 9 are 2, 4, 6 and 8.
2 + 4 + 6 + 8 = 20

**6) C**
C is the only shape that has only one line of symmetry.

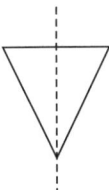

**7) 15**
Each sweet symbol on the pictogram shows 6 sweets. There are 2 and a half symbols shown for strawberry laces. Half a symbol = 6 ÷ 2 = 3 sweets. So the number of strawberry laces sold was 6 + 6 + 3 = 15.

**8) 8**
¼ of 32 is the same as 32 ÷ 4 = 8. So ¼ of 32 is 8.

**9) D**
For each child to be able to have one of each type of book, there needs to be 24 of each book. Look at which bars reach 24 books on the vertical axis. Both the History and English bars on the chart are below 24, so there aren't enough of these types of books.

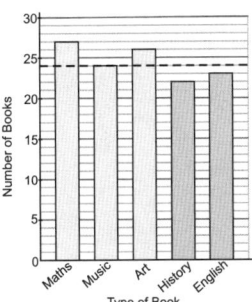

**10) C**
There are 100 cm in 1 m, so to convert 17.04 m into centimetres you multiply by 100: 17.04 × 100 = 1704 cm.

**11) 31 °C**
Count up from −5 to 26 to
find the difference between them.

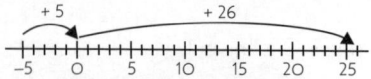

Add 5 to get from −5 to 0.
Add 26 to get from 0 to 26.
5 + 26 = 31 °C

**12) 9**
54 ÷ 6 = 9, so 54 children could be split to make 9 teams
of 6. That would leave two children left over (56 − 54 = 2),
which isn't enough to make another complete team.

**13) C**
The number that goes into section X has to be a
multiple of 7 and 4. Only 28 is a multiple of both
4 and 7 (4 × 7 = 28, 7 × 4 = 28).

**14) 7.6**
The space between 7 and 8 is split into 10 gaps — each gap
is worth one tenth (0.1). The arrow is pointing at a line 6
gaps further along than 7, which must have a value of 6 tenths
greater than 7. 7 + 0.6 = 7.6

**15) D**
First look at the number of minutes shown by each clock —
only clocks B, C and D match (they each show 35 minutes).
The hour hand on clock B is between 6 and 7 so it shows 6:35.
The time shown on clock D is in the 24-hour clock — subtract
12 from the number of hours to find the time in the 12-hour
clock: 18 − 12 = 6. So the time on clock D is 6:35, which
is the same as on clock B.

**16) D**
74 is being rounded to the nearest 10. 75 is halfway between
70 and 80. 74 is less than 75, so 74 rounds down to 70.
Hemish is the only child who has a rounded score of 70, so
Hemish could have scored 74 on the test.

**17) C**
You need to look for the shapes that have an equal amount
of shading. ⁴⁄₁₀ of shape A is shaded and ²⁄₅ of shape B is
shaded. The diagrams below have been rearranged to show
that the shapes have the same amount shaded, and so the
fractions are the same.

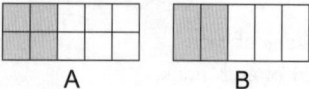

**18) C**
Find the highest number below 5000, and the lowest number
above 5000 — one of these will be the closest number to
5000. Then just work out the difference between 5000 and
these two numbers.
Highest number below 5000 = 4972
Lowest number above 5000 = 5029
5000 − 4972 = 28, 5029 − 5000 = 29.
So 4972 is closest.

**19) D**
A right angle is 90°. Angle *a* is smaller than a
right angle so it's less than 90°. The only option
that is less than 90° is 45°.

**20) £6.93**
Round up 99p to £1 and multiply by 7: 7 × £1 = £7.
You added an extra 1p to each price, so in total you added
7 × 1p = 7p extra. Subtract this from your rounded answer to
find the correct price: £7.00 − 7p = £6.93

**21) 70p**
Subtract the cost of a loaf of bread from the total cost to find
the cost of the three cans of cola: £3.00 − 90p
= 300p − 90p = 210p. Divide 210p by 3 to find the price of
each can of cola. 21 ÷ 3 = 7. 210 is ten times bigger than 21,
so 210 ÷ 3 will be 10 times bigger than 7. That means the
price of a can of cola is 7 × 10 = 70p

**22) B**
The number with the missing digit is multiplied by 8 to give
120. So 120 divided by 8 must equal this number (because
dividing is the opposite of multiplying).
You can partition 120 into two smaller numbers and
then divide each number by 8. 120 splits into 80 + 40.
80 ÷ 8 = 10, 40 ÷ 8 = 5. 10 + 5 = 15.
So 15 × 8 = 120, which means the missing digit is 5.

**23) B**
Imagine folding the net along the dotted lines and work out
which edges of the net will join together. This net will fold up to
be a prism with triangular faces at both ends. So it will make a
triangular prism.

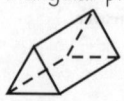

**24) B**
A rectangle can only be split into
two triangles by cutting it like this:
This means each triangle will have
a right angle — so option B is correct.

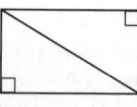

**25) D**
Count down from 13 in steps of 4 until you reach one of the
options.

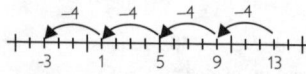

**26) D**
Add up the number of pounds raised by each stall during the
day to find the total amount collected by each stall.
Tombola: 18 + 11 = £29
Coconut Shy: 15 + 17 = £32
Penalty Shoot-out: 16 + 22 = £38
Pony Ride: 21 + 19 = £40
Bash the Rat: 13 + 20 = £33
So Pony Ride collected the most money.

**27) 50p**
Esther paid £36 for 100 ice pops. So the amount she
paid for each ice pop = £36 ÷ 100, which is the same
as 3600p ÷ 100 = 36p. Add 14p to find the price
she charges for each ice pop. 36p + 14p = 50p

**28) 6**
Work backwards through Sasha's calculation to find the
number she started with. She adds 3 to a number to get 51,
so subtract 3 from 51: 51 − 3 = 48. 48 is the start number
multiplied by 8. So divide by 8 to find Sasha's
start number: 48 ÷ 8 = 6.

**29) A**

Multiply the number of stick lengths by the length of the stick to find the length of the playground in centimetres: 30 × 55 cm. You could partition 55 into 50 + 5 to make the multiplication easier. 30 × 50 + 30 × 5 = 1500 + 150 = 1650 cm. 1 m = 100 cm, so divide by 100 to find the length in metres: 1650 ÷ 100 = 16.5 m.

**30) B**

The shape is a rectangle so it has two pairs of equal sides. This means that the *x*-coordinate of corner D is the same as corner C (8). The *y*-coordinate of corner D is the same as corner A (4). So the coordinates of corner D are (8, 4).

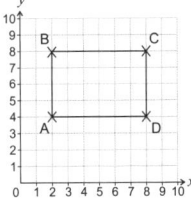

# Assessment Test 5

## Pages 57-61

**1) 5**

There's no number that can go into the middle section of this Venn diagram because a number can't be both odd and even.

**2) D**

A shape with 5 equal sides is a regular pentagon.

**3) A**

There are 72 passengers in total and each minibus can hold 9 passengers. So the number of minibuses needed is 72 ÷ 9 = 8.

**4) 300 g**

There are 5 spaces on the scale between 0 kg and 500 g, so each space on the scale is worth 100 g. The arrow is pointing 3 spaces from 0 kg, so the weight of the sugar is 3 × 100 g = 300 g.

**5) C**

850 mm and 85 cm are the same and both less than 1 m. An adult is usually between 1.5 m and 1.8 m tall, so these measurements are too small to be the height of a house. 80.5 m is roughly the height of a tower block, and 0.85 km is the same as 850 m, so both of these heights are far taller than a house — 8.5 m is the only realistic answer.

**6) D**

< means 'is less than', so the numbers in the shaded box must be even numbers that are less than 10. 6 and 8 are both even and less than 10, so D is the correct answer.

**7) C**

The circle is split into 12 parts and 7 parts are shaded. As a fraction this is 7/12.

**8) C**

35 is a multiple of 5 (5 × 7 = 35) but it's not a multiple of 3.

**9) 17.5 m**

17.45 is halfway between 17.4 and 17.5. 17.48 is more than 17.45, so 17.48 rounds up to 17.5 m.

**10) A**

100p ÷ 20p = 5, so there are five 20p coins in £1. The weight of the coins will be 5 × 5 g = 25 g.

**11) D**

You can work this out by partitioning 567 into 500 + 60 + 7 and then subtracting each number from 1000 one at a time. 1000 − 500 = 500, 500 − 60 = 440, 440 − 7 = 433.

**12) E**

Count back from −7 °C. 3 °C takes you to −10 °C and 2 °C takes you to −12 °C.

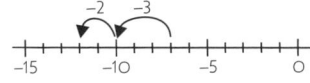

3 °C + 2 °C = 5 °C.

**13) 560**

The missing number is divided by 8 to give 70. So 70 × 8 must equal the missing number (because multiplying is the opposite of dividing). You know that 7 × 8 = 56. 70 is ten times larger than 7, so the answer will be ten times larger: 56 × 10 = 560. So 560 ÷ 8 = 70.

**14) 9 points**

Each symbol on the pictogram shows 6 points. There are 2 symbols for Team 2, so they have 2 × 6 = 12 points. There are 3½ symbols for Team 5. ½ of 6 is 3 and 3 × 6 = 18. So Team 5 have 3 + 18 = 21 points. So the difference between the two teams is 21 − 12 = 9 points. (Or you could work out that Team 5 has 1½ symbols more than Team 2. ½ symbol = 6 ÷ 2 = 3, so the difference = 6 + 3 = 9 points.)

**15) D**

Count on from 8:57 to 10:45. 8:57 to 9:00 is 3 minutes. 9:00 to 10:00 is 1 hour. 10:00 to 10:45 is 45 minutes. 1 hour + 45 minutes + 3 minutes = 1 hour and 48 minutes.

**16) B**

There are three 3 kg blocks so that would be 3 × 3 = 9 kg in total. 1 kg = 1000 g. So 9 kg is 9 × 1000 = 9000 g.

**17) A**

3 squares down takes you to (4, 3). 2 squares right takes you to (6, 3).

**18) 6**

The previous number has been doubled to give 12. So find half of 12 to find the previous number: 12 ÷ 2 = 6.

**19) A**

Imagine folding each of the nets and work out which edges will join together. Net A is the only net that will fold up to make a cube.

**20) C**

The diagram shows shape X being reflected. Option C is the reflected shape.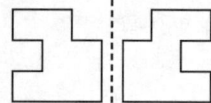

**21) D**

There are 100 cm in 1 m, so you need to work out 100 ÷ 7. You can solve this by partitioning 100 into 70 + 30 and dividing each number by 7. Then you add together the results.
70 ÷ 7 = 10, 30 ÷ 7 = 4 r 2. 10 + 4 r 2 = 14 r 2.
So that means you can fit 14 books on the bookshelf, and there will be 2 cm of space left over.

**22) 35 m**

Building 3 is 90 metres tall and building 5 is 55 metres tall. So building 3 is 90 − 55 = 35 metres taller than building 5.

**23) B**

Round 49p up to 50p. 4 × 50p = £2.00. You added an extra 1p to each price, so in total you added 4 × 1p = 4p. Subtract 4p from your rounded answer to find the actual cost of 4 oranges: £2.00 − 4p = £1.96. Subtract £1.96 from £10 to work out the change that Kaya is given: £10 − £1.96 = £8.04.

**24) A**

Each cube has 6 faces so there are 6 × 6 = 36 faces in total on the 6 cubes. There are 5 cubes which are attached by one face to the cube in the centre, so 5 faces of each of those cubes are painted blue: 5 × 5 = 25 blue faces in total. The cube in the centre has 5 of its faces attached to 5 cubes, so only one of its faces would be painted blue. There are 25 + 1 = 26 blue faces in total. That means there are 36 − 26 = 10 white faces.

**25) B**

There are 1000 ml in 1 litre so there is 3 × 1000 = 3000 ml of water in the jug. The amount of water Maxine pours into glasses is 6 × 200 ml = 1200 ml. This means that there is 3000 − 1200 = 1800 ml left in the jug.

**26) C**

A square-based pyramid has one square face and four triangular faces.

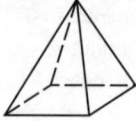

**27) 69**

Each chapter is 8 pages long, so the first 8 chapters will be 8 × 8 = 64 pages long. She has also read 5 pages of chapter 9, so in total she has read 5 + 64 = 69 pages.

**28) D**

There are 7 days in a week, so the cat eats 7 × 85 g of tinned meat each week. You can use partitioning to solve this calculation. Split 85 into 80 + 5 and multiply each number by 7. Then add together the results. 80 × 7 = 560, 5 × 7 = 35. 560 + 35 = 595 g.

**29) D**

There are 24 hours in 1 day so there are 2 × 24 = 48 hours in 2 days. So 50 hours is 2 days and 2 hours. Count on 2 hours from 9 am on Sunday to get to 11 am. Then count on 2 days to get to 11 am on Tuesday. So the battery will need to be charged at 11 am on Tuesday.

**30) B**

To make a right angle, Harvey needs to draw a horizontal line from point B. This means that the point needs to have the same y-coordinate as point B (2). The only possible option is (3, 2).

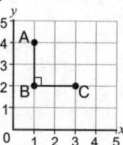

# Assessment Test 6

## Pages 62-66

**1) 134**

Look at the place value of the first digit in each of the numbers given. Both 113 and 134 have 1 hundred. Then look at the place value of the second digit in the next column on the right.
113 has 1 ten, and 134 has 3 tens. So 134 is the biggest number.

**2) March**

The month with the highest amount of rain will have the tallest bar — March.

**3) D**

Break up 110 into 100 + 10 and subtract each part from 1000. 1000 − 10 = 990, 990 − 100 = 890.

**4) 28**

Add up the 7 digits carefully, one at a time, so you don't make any mistakes. 0 + 5 + 1 + 5 + 6 + 4 + 7 = 28

**5) B**

Subtract 149 from 606 to find the number of chickens at Shrove Farm. You could do this by counting back from 606 to 149, then adding up the numbers you counted back.
606 − 6 = 600, 600 − 400 = 20, 200 − 50 = 150,
150 − 1 = 149, 6 + 400 + 50 + 1 = 457.
Alternately you could partition 149 and subtract each number from 606. 149 splits into 100 + 40 + 9.
606 − 9 = 597, 597 − 40 = 557, 557 − 100 = 457.

**6) C**

Look for the biggest number under 3 kg and the smallest number above 3 kg. Then look at the difference between 3 kg and these two numbers. The difference between 2.9 kg and 3 kg is 3 − 2.9 = 0.1 kg. The difference between 3.2 kg and 3 kg is 3.2 − 3 = 0.2 kg. So 2.9 kg is closest to 3 kg.

**7) 2 hours**

Each symbol on the pictogram shows 4 hours of sunshine. There are 1½ symbols for Monday. ½ of 4 is 2 and 1 × 4 = 4. So there were 2 + 4 = 6 hours of sunshine in total. There are 2 symbols for Thursday, so there were 2 × 4 = 8 hours of sunshine in total. The difference between the number of hours of sunshine on Monday and Thursday is: 8 − 6 = 2.
(Or, you could work out that there's a difference of half a symbol on the pictogram. 1 symbol = 4 hours, so half a symbol = 4 ÷ 2 = 2 hours).

**8) D**

The difference between 58 and 71 is 13. 58 + 13 = 71

**9) E**

To work out the position of each square you count across the horizontal axis until you find the letter. Then you count up the vertical axis until you find the number. F7 is not inside the triangle.

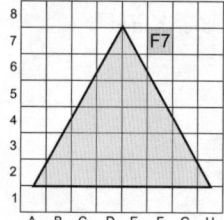

**10) B**
Count back in 5s from 17 until you reach one of the options:
17, 12, 7, 2... 2 is the only option that's in the sequence.

**11) 35**
35 is an odd number and a multiple of 7 (7 × 5 = 35).
It should be in the middle section of the Venn diagram.

**12) C**
57 minutes is only 3 minutes less than 1 hour. So add an hour and then subtract 3 minutes to find the finish time. 1 hour on from 17:45 is 18:45, and 3 minutes back from 18:45 is 18:42.

**13) C**
You know from your times tables that 8 × 4 = 32, so 32 ÷ 4 = 8. 320 is ten times larger than 32, so the answer will be ten times larger: 320 ÷ 4 = 80 beads.

**14) A**
Count the number of squares inside the shape to find its area. The area of each square is 1 cm$^2$ and there are 22 squares inside the shape, so the area of the shape is 22 cm$^2$.

**15) B**
115 is halfway between 110 and 120.
117 is more than 115, so 117 rounds up
to 120 when rounded to the nearest 10.

**16) 30 cm**
The rectangles are all the same so the length of every long side is 3 cm and the length of every short side is 2 cm.
So the perimeter of the shape is:
3 + 2 + 3 + 2 + 3 + 2 + 3 + 2 + 3 + 2 + 3 + 2 = 30 cm.

**17) B**
The total cost of three postcards is 3 × 40p = £1.20.
Subtract £1.20 from £5 to work out the amount of change she receives. Partition £1.20 into £1 + 20p and subtract each number one at a time: £5 − £1 = £4, £4 − 20p = £3.80.
So Nikki receives £3.80 in change.

**18) E**
9 × 9 = 81. 90 is ten times larger than 9,
so the answer will be ten times larger: 81 × 10 = 810.

**19) E**
½ is equal to 0.5.

**20) 12 litres**
The car needs 2 litres of fuel to travel 12 miles, so it will need 12 ÷ 2 = 6 litres of fuel to travel 1 mile. You then need to work out 72 ÷ 6 — you could do this by partitioning 72 into 60 and 12. 60 ÷ 6 = 10, and 12 ÷ 6 = 2.
So the car needs 10 + 2 = 12 litres of fuel to travel 72 miles.

**21) 20 cm**
Read off the values for weeks 4, 5 and 6, then add them together to find the total growth. 5 + 7 + 8 = 20 cm.

**22) A**
Ada gives away ⅕ of 15 marbles. ⅕ of 15 is the same as 15 ÷ 5 = 3. The number of marbles that Ada has left is 15 − 3 = 12 marbles.

**23) B**
The diagram below shows the reflected rectangle.
The reflection of point Z is at point B.

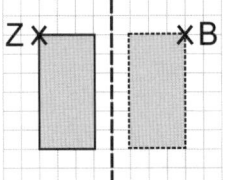

**24) D**
In Jug A there is 1.5 litres of orange juice.
There are 1000 ml in 1 litre, so to convert this into millilitres you multiply by 1000: 1.5 × 1000 = 1500 ml. There are 2000 ml in Jug B, so add this to the amount in Jug A to find the total amount of juice: 1500 + 2000 = 3500 ml.

**25) E**
Imagine folding each of the nets and work out which edges will join together. Net E is the only net that will fold up to make a square-based pyramid.

**26) D**
The difference between −16 °C and −9 °C is 7 °C.
The temperature rises 1 °C every hour, so it will take 7 hours to rise 7 °C. 7 hours on from 4 am is 11 am.

**27) A**
A cube has 6 faces. The shape is made up of 5 cubes in total. Each cube that is stuck to the cube in the centre has 1 face with glue on, so they have 6 − 1 = 5 faces without glue on them. There are four of these cubes, so there are a total of 5 × 4 = 20 faces without glue on them. The cube in the centre is attached to 4 cubes so it has glue on 4 faces. This means that it has 6 − 4 = 2 faces without glue on them. So in total there are 20 + 2 = 22 faces without glue on them.

**28) £76.00**
You can solve this by partitioning. Break up £9.50 into £9 + 50p and multiply each part by 8 separately.
£9 × 8 = £72, 50p × 8 = £4.00. Add the two values together to find the cost of 8 tickets: £72 + £4.00 = £76.00.

**29) 225 g**
Subtract the weight of the cheese from the total weight to find the weight of the 2 packs of butter: 920 g − 470 g = 450 g.
Divide the total weight of the 2 packs of butter by 2 to find the weight of 1 pack of butter: 450 g ÷ 2 = 225 g.

**30) 11**
There are two ways to work out the answer to this question:
1) Find the number of girls in Year 5 by subtracting the number of boys in Year 5 from the total number of children in Year 5: 26 − 9 = 17. Then subtract the number of girls in Year 5 from the total number of girls to find the number of girls in Year 4: 28 − 17 = 11.
2) Find the number of children in Year 4 by subtracting the number of children in Year 5 from the total number of children on the trip: 59 − 26 = 33. Then subtract the number of boys in Year 4 from the total number of children in Year 4 to find the number of girls: 33 − 22 = 11.

# Progress Chart

Use this chart to keep track of your scores for the Assessment Tests.

You can do each test more than once — download extra answer sheets from cgpbooks.co.uk/11plus/answer-sheets or scan the QR code on the right.

Answer Sheets

|  | First Go | Second Go | Third Go |
|---|---|---|---|
| Test 1 | Date: <br> Score: | Date: <br> Score: | Date: <br> Score: |
| Test 2 | Date: <br> Score: | Date: <br> Score: | Date: <br> Score: |
| Test 3 | Date: <br> Score: | Date: <br> Score: | Date: <br> Score: |
| Test 4 | Date: <br> Score: | Date: <br> Score: | Date: <br> Score: |
| Test 5 | Date: <br> Score: | Date: <br> Score: | Date: <br> Score: |
| Test 6 | Date: <br> Score: | Date: <br> Score: | Date: <br> Score: |

Look back at your scores once you've done all the Assessment Tests.
Each test is out of 30 marks.

Work out which kind of mark you scored most often:

**0-18 marks** — Go back to basics and work on your question technique.

**19-25 marks** — You're nearly there — go back over the questions you found tricky.

**26-30 marks** — You're a Maths star. Go on to Practice Book Age 9-10.